Fun with Your Microscope

**SHAR LEVINE &
LESLIE JOHNSTONE**

*Illustrations by
Jason Coons*

Photomicrographs by
James Humphrey
& the authors

Sterling Publishing Co., Inc.
New York

To my husband, Paul Rosenberg, on the occasion of our twentieth anniversary. You have given me love, happiness and laughter over the last two decades.—S. L.

To my husband, Mark Johnstone, with much love and affection.—L. J.

For Pete, Ben, Ma, and Pa. I love you all. "He's still cutting!"—J. C.

The authors wish to express their gratitude to Dr. Elaine Humphrey, Ellen Rosenberg, Rufus Guitars, Melissa and Lawrence Davidson of Bean Bros. Coffee, Gerri York, Charles Nurnberg, Isabel Stein, and the law firm of Rosenberg and Rosenberg.
Photo credits: Photomicrographs by James Humphrey and the authors. The microscope pictured on the cover was provided by Carolina Biological Supply Co., Burlington, North Carolina.

Designed by Judy Morgan; edited by Isabel Stein

Library of Congress Cataloging-in-Publication Data

Levine, Shar, 1953–
    Fun with your microscope / by Shar Levine and Leslie Johnstone; illustrations by Jason Coons; photomicrographs by James Humphrey and the authors.
        p.   cm.
    Includes index.
    Summary: Presents basic techniques for using a microscope to observe and investigate a variety of materials that might be found around the house. Also includes experiments and ideas for science fair projects.
    ISBN 0-8069-9945-4
    1. Microscopy—Juvenile literature. 2. Microscopes—Juvenile literature. [1. Microscopy—Experiments. 2. Microscopes. 3. Experiments.]   I. Johnstone, Leslie.   II. Coons, Jason, ill.   III. Humphrey, James.   IV. Title.
QH278.L47   1997
502'.8'2—dc21   97-27609
                                                                                                            CIP
                                                                                                            AC

1   3   5   7   9   10   8   6   4   2

First paperback edition published in 1999 by
Sterling Publishing Company, Inc.
387 Park Avenue South, New York, N.Y. 10016
© 1998 by Shar Levine & Leslie Johnstone
Distributed in Canada by Sterling Publishing
℅ Canadian Manda Group, One Atlantic Avenue, Suite 105
Toronto, Ontario, Canada M6K 3E7
Distributed in Great Britain and Europe by Chris Lloyd
463 Ashley Road, Parkstone Poole, Dorset BH14 0AX, England
Distributed in Australia by Capricorn Link (Australia) Pty Ltd.
P.O. Box 6651, Baulkham Hills, Business Centre, NSW 2153, Australia
Printed in Hong Kong
All rights reserved

Sterling ISBN   0-8069-9945-4 Trade
                        0-8069-9946-2 Paper

Contents

Preface

Some of the things you handle every day look strange, even eerie, under the microscope. The bottom of a mushroom looks like delicate threads of fabric. The cells of a leaf look like an aerial map of a strange country. And you may not want to even look at the stuff growing on a sponge in your kitchen!

Welcome to the world of microscopes. There are all sorts of new and fun things to see and try in dozens of experiments. Learn about bacteria by viewing sauerkraut, yogurt, and the guck between your teeth. Find out what items are hidden in the money in your pocket. Join us on a hunt for the "little man" inside Lincoln's tomb on an American penny! All these things are possible, even if you only have an inexpensive microscope on hand.

Following each experiment are ideas that you might want to consider developing for a science fair or school project.

You'll learn basic slide-making techniques. (A slide is a sample prepared for viewing on a thin, rectangular piece of glass.) Microscopes may look complicated, but they aren't! Using these simple step-by-step instructions, you'll be an expert in no time. The skills and procedures you need to know are described in the Microscope Basics section of the book. The experiments can be done with easy-to-get foods and other supplies and materials you find around the house. We have not used any special stains or hard-to-find chemicals in this book. If you don't understand a particular word, you probably can find it in the glossary.

If you find that your slide looks different from the one shown in the book, don't fret. Try to make several slides and see if one more closely resembles the picture. We made all the slides using the same techniques we described in this book, but some of our slides may be clearer because we may have used a better microscope than you are using. Some were made with colored filters so that you can see them clearly. The color may be different than what you see on your slide.

When you finish this book, you probably will want to learn more. Your library probably has many books on microscopes. Ask a librarian for help in finding them. Some books you read may recommend other chemicals or stains. Before you use any chemicals, make sure to get the permission of and help from an adult, as some are very poisonous.

Many great scientists got their start on microscopes less complicated than yours. Keep a journal to remind you of what you saw and learned. Who knows . . . someday, when you are accepting the Nobel Prize for Biochemistry or Medicine, you can think back to your humble beginnings with a simple microscope! Good luck and happy experimenting.

NOTE TO PARENTS AND TEACHERS

The microscopic world is fascinating to children of all ages. They are delighted to learn that there is a whole world in a single slide. Children will happily spend hours peering through a microscope. Ask children what they'd like to see close up.

We've tried to make the experiments as safe and fool-proof as possible. Where sharp tools are needed, we suggest that the child have an adult helper. The Microscope Basics section of the book explains the function of each part of the microscope and covers other basic concepts and slide techniques. Scientific words are defined the first time they are used; many also appear in the glossary at the back of the book.

Fun with Your Microscope is intended to teach children basic techniques and observation skills. We do not recommend growing any bacterial cultures or using human blood to make slides, which can be dangerous if not handled correctly. There are many safe experiments and wonderful things to view under a microscope.

Encourage children to keep a journal of the things they see through the microscope. If you are a teacher, have the class write a report on the different kinds of microscopes that were developed through the ages, or have students bring in magazine photos made with an electron microscope.

If you do not own a microscope, don't despair. A magnifying glass can be used to perform some of the experiments in this book. If you are looking for a microscope, note that universities and some microscope companies sell off their used microscopes. Call the purchasing department and ask if there are any microscopes for sale.

Universities and colleges may also offer tours of their science and research facilities. You can organize a field trip for your class to see a powerful microscope in action.

Be prepared for squeals of delight as children peer through a microscope and discover a whole new world.

SAFETY FIRST

Before you begin any of the activities in this book, there are a few do's and don'ts you need to know so that you can use your microscope safely.

Do's

1. Ask an adult before handling any materials, food, or equipment.

2. Have an adult do the tasks involving all sharp objects, such as knives or razor blades. When you see the ⚠ symbol, it means sharp tools or other sharp objects are used.

3. Read all the steps of any experiment carefully, assemble your supplies, and be sure you know what to do before you begin the experiment.

4. Always work in a well-ventilated area with good lighting.

5. Tie back long hair while you work, and avoid wearing clothing with long, loose sleeves, which could knock things over.

6. Keep your work area clean, and wipe up any spills immediately.

7. Wash your hands and your work area after doing the experiments.

8. Tell an adult immediately if you hurt yourself in any way.

9. Keep all supplies, tools, chemicals, and experiments out of the reach of very young children.

Don'ts

1. If you are allergic to or sensitive to any substances, such as dust or pollen, do not use them to perform experiments.

2. Do not taste, eat, or drink any of the experiments.

3. Do not be cruel to any living creatures in your experiments.

4. Never look at the sun or another strong light source through your magnifying lens or microscope.

List of Equipment

Before you get started, have the following basic supplies and equipment handy. If you need extra slides or scientific supplies, check in the yellow pages of your telephone book under Scientific Instruments, or look in scientific supply catalogs and toy stores. Gather together all the materials that you need for an experiment and read each experiment through before you start slicing the samples. Make sure you have an adult's permission before using any sharp objects or handling any equipment.

YOU WILL NEED

➜ microscope
➜ slides
➜ cover slips (cover glasses)
➜ tweezers
➜ eyedropper
➜ tincture of iodine
➜ facial tissues
➜ lens paper
➜ notebook
➜ pen and pencil
➜ colored pencils
➜ stage micrometer or clear plastic ruler
➜ compass or jar lid for drawing circles
➜ homemade microtome*
➜ craft knife or industrial (single-edged) razor blade
➜ magnifying glass
➜ petroleum jelly

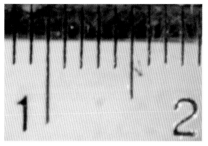

Clear plastic ruler. The short lines actually are 1 mm apart.

➜ clear colorless nail polish
➜ scissors
➜ paper toweling
➜ food coloring
➜ sharp pins
➜ India ink
➜ teaspoon
➜ table lamp
➜ cellophane tape

*See page 11 for supplies needed to make a microtome and instructions.

Microscope Basics

Before you get started, we'll go over some information and techniques you will need to do the experiments. First we'll cover the basic parts of the microscope and their functions. If you aren't experienced, don't worry; there isn't a test. We'll describe some basic slide-making techniques also.

It may be tempting to flip through the book to your favorite slide, but make sure you understand how your microscope works and how slides are made before you jump ahead. Spending 10 minutes learning a basic technique will save you hours of time later. If you are unsure of a technique or you need help with any of the equipment, ask an adult for assistance.

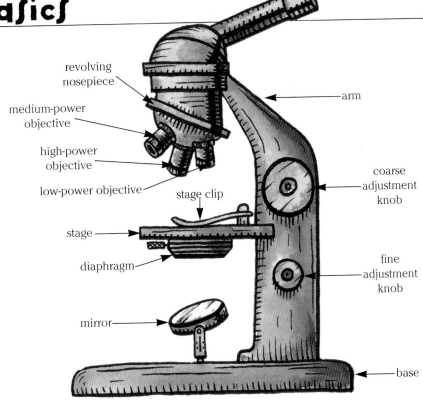

PARTS OF A MICROSCOPE

A. The eyepiece (ocular) is the part of the microscope closest to your eye, through which you look. It contains the ocular lens, which makes the image produced by the objective's lenses larger. Microscopes in which separate images are seen by each of the observer's eyes at the same time are called binocular microscopes. An eyepiece may be labeled with its magnification or power—for example, 5✕ (meaning the eyepiece enlarges 5 times). Your microscope may even have a view screen or an attached projector that acts as an ocular lens.

B. The tube holds the eyepiece in position over the revolving nosepiece and the objectives. The tube can be straight up and down or slanted.

C. The arm is the curved metal piece that holds the body tube in place over the stage and the base.

D. The revolving nosepiece holds the objectives and allows you to change objectives while looking at a slide.

E. The objectives are the parts at the bottom of the body tube, closest to the sample you are examining. Each objective has a lens and a tubelike holder, the mount. Like the eyepieces, objectives come in various powers. The longer mounts hold the stronger lenses (the high-power lenses). The shorter mounts hold the weaker lenses (the low-power lenses). Some microscopes have several objectives (for example, 4✕, 10✕, 40✕ and 100✕); some only have one or two.

F. The stage is the flat surface on which you put your slides or samples.

G. The stage clips hold the slides in place on the stage. Some microscopes have a moveable stage, on which the slides are held in place by moveable jaws.

H. The diaphragm is used to adjust the amount of light shining through the sample on the stage. (Some microscopes do not have diaphragms.)

I. The coarse adjustment knob is the large knob used to roughly adjust the position of the body tube, allowing you to quickly bring your sample into view.

J. The fine adjustment knob is the small knob used to change the position of the body tube, allowing you to make small adjustments to the focus of your sample. Most microscopes have both a coarse and a fine adjustment knob, but some only have one knob.

K. The mirror or lamp, located beneath the stage and diaphragm, increases the amount of light shining through your sample. The lamp may be battery-powered or it may plug into an electrical outlet.

L. Beneath the stage, some microscopes have a condenser, which collects and concentrates the light before it passes through the sample.

M. The base of the microscope is the heavy bottom part. It supports all the other parts of the microscope.

Units of Measurement

Microscopists look at objects that are very, very tiny. Like other scientists, they use a system of measurement known as the International System of Units, or SI, based on the metric system. The metric system uses multiples of 10 and is based on a standard length of 1 meter. Microscopic objects are usually measured in either millimeters (mm) or micrometers (μm). A millimeter is 1/1000 of a meter. A micrometer is 1/1000 of a millimeter. Microscopic objects can be measured using a slide with a built-in ruler called a stage micrometer. Some metric units that we need are given here, as well as some conversions to metric units from the common units used in the United States and Great Britain.

Metric Units	From Common to Metric Units
1 meter (m) = 100 centimeters (cm)	1 yard = 0.91 meter (m)
1 meter = 1000 millimeters (mm)	1 foot = 30.48 centimeters (cm)
1 meter = 1 000 000 micrometers (μm)	1 inch = 2.54 centimeters (cm)
1 centimeter = 10 millimeters (mm)	1 cup = .24 liter (L)
1 centimeter = 10 000 micrometers (μm)	1 fluid ounce = 30 milliliters (mL)
1 millimeter = 1000 micrometers (μm)	1 teaspoon = 5 milliliters (mL)
1 liter (L) = 1000 milliliters (mL)	1 tablespoon = 15 milliliters (mL)

FOCUSING

There are a few simple rules to follow to avoid damaging your microscope or your slides.

1. Remove your microscope from its box or cover. Always pick up your microscope correctly: grasp it firmly with two hands, one hand under the base and the other on the arm.

2. Place the microscope on a table, away from the edge. Move it to a position in which you can look comfortably through the eyepiece. You may want to sit on a chair or stool.

3. Make sure the low-power objective is in place over the hole in the stage. Use the coarse adjustment knob to raise the objective so its lowest end is about 1 inch (2.5 cm) above the stage.

4. Place your sample on the stage and carefully secure it with stage clips. Do not snap the stage clips, as you could damage the clips or the sample. Adjust the position of your sample so that it is over the hole in the stage.

5. Adjust your mirror or other light source to focus light through the sample. You should be able to see a circle of light when you look into the eye-piece. Never use your microscope in direct sunlight, as the reflected light could damage your eyes. If your microscope has a lamp, turn it on. You may need to replace the batteries or plug the lamp into an electrical outlet, depending on the style of microscope you have. When viewing very thick samples, you may have to shine light on the sample from above by using a table lamp or by placing your microscope in a brightly lit place.

6. Look at the objective from the side, and use the coarse adjustment knob to lower the objective as close as possible to the sample.

7. Look through the eyepiece and use the coarse adjustment knob to focus upwards (moving away from the sample). This should bring the sample into view. If you go too far, simply begin again at step 6.

8. When the sample is in view, use the fine adjustment knob to bring it clearly into focus. If necessary, slide the sample gently sideways to bring it into the center of your field of view.

9. To use the high-power objective, turn the revolving nose-piece to bring the objective into position over your sample. You

Magnification

The markings on the objectives and eyepieces of your microscope tell you their magnifying power, how many times bigger they make the samples appear. If the eyepiece has the marking 10× on it, it means that if it were used on its own, the objects you would see would appear to be 10 times bigger than they actually are. To calculate the magnification of the things you are looking at, multiply the power of the eyepiece by the power of the objective. If you use the 10× eyepiece with a low-power objective marked 4×, you will see objects that are magnified $10 \times 4 = 40$ times (40×). A 40× objective with a 10× eyepiece will magnify objects 400 times.

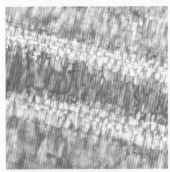

Grass blade at 125×; enlarged.

should be able to see the sample through the high-power objective, so you will only have to adjust the fine adjustment knob. Remember to always focus upwards so that the objective is moving away from the sample. Focusing downwards could break your slide or damage your lens.

10. Return to the low-power objective before removing the sample from the stage. To look at another sample, repeat steps 3 through 9.

11. When you are finished using the microscope, make sure the low-power objective is in position over the hole in the stage and turn off the light.

12. If your lenses get dirty, you may see spots or smudges when you look through the microscope, even if no sample is present. To clean them, always use lens paper, which you can purchase at a camera store. Tissue paper or cloth could damage your lenses. Breathe onto the surface of the lens and wipe in a circular motion.

STORAGE

Store your microscope, covered with a box or bag, where it won't be knocked over. Use a plastic grocery bag, if neces-

sary, and label the bag or box. Remove the batteries from your microscope, if it has batteries, when you store it. Make sure you support the box or bag when moving the microscope.

Label and store your slides in a safe place. If you are not making permanent slides, wash and dry the slides thoroughly after you are finished using them, and put them back in a box. Do not leave slides or cover glasses on the floor or on a table as they may break and hurt people.

KEEPING A JOURNAL

Scientists write down information about their experiments so that they know what they did and what happened as a result. When you look at samples with your microscope, keep a record of your work in a notebook or on large index cards. Create your own journal log or photocopy the blank form given here.

DATE SAMPLE GATHERED: _____ DATE OF SLIDE: _____

WHAT SAMPLE IS: _____

WHERE SAMPLE IS FROM: _____

HOW SAMPLE WAS PREPARED: _____

METHOD: _____

STAINS: _____

MOUNT: _____

OBJECTIVE / EYEPIECE USED: _____

LIGHTING USED: _____

OBSERVATIONS: _____

_____

_____

_____

ESTIMATED SIZE OF SAMPLE: _____

DRAWING OF SAMPLE:

Here are some other procedures and techniques you will need to use for the experiments in this book.

MAKING AND USING A MICROTOME ⚠️

A microtome is a piece of equipment that helps you to make very thin slices (sections) of samples. A very thin section lets light through, so you can see the structure of your sample easily. Here's how you can make your own microtome.

You Will Need

→ empty thread spool with a hole 3⁄16 inch (5 mm) in diameter

→ metal nut and bolt about 3⁄16 inch (5 mm) in diameter

→ ice cream stick

→ waterproof glue that will stick metal to wood

→ fine-point waterproof marking pen

→ specimen

→ carrot

→ razor knife or single-edged razor blade

→ small bowl and water

→ tweezers and microscope

→ slide and cover slip

→ adult helper

nut glued to spool

glue ice cream stick to head of bolt

lines help you know how much to turn to push up the same amount of sample each time

Steps in microtome construction.

A. Thread the metal bolt through the empty thread spool and screw on the nut. Carefully remove the bolt and have an adult attach the nut to the spool using waterproof glue. Allow the glue to set.

B. Have an adult glue the head of the bolt to the middle of the flat side of an ice cream stick. Allow the glue to set. The ice cream stick acts as your handle.

C. Screw the metal nut and spool onto the bolt. Do not tighten the bolt; thread it on, leaving a space at the top for your sample.

D. Use a fine-point waterproof marking pen to draw eight

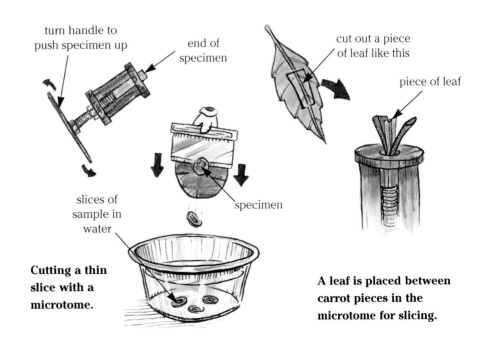

turn handle to push specimen up

end of specimen

cut out a piece of leaf like this

piece of leaf

slices of sample in water

specimen

Cutting a thin slice with a microtome.

A leaf is placed between carrot pieces in the microtome for slicing.

equally spaced lines around the flat bottom surface of the spool (see drawing). These markings will help you to know how far to turn the stick so you can make each section you cut the same thickness. You are now ready to use your microtome.

E. Have an adult cut your sample to fit inside the hole in the top of the spool with nothing sticking out. A piece of carrot can be used to fill in any empty spaces or support oddly shaped samples. Turn the handle of your microtome to raise the carrot and sample a bit.

F. Have an adult slice across the top of your sample with a craft knife or single-edged razor blade. Dip the blade and the section into a bowl of water. The section should float off the blade. Turn the handle and cut another section. Repeat the dipping and cutting until you have several sections.

G. Use tweezers to transfer your sections to slides. Make a wet mount.

MAKING A WET MOUNT

You will need: your sample, water, tweezers, slide and cover slip, paper towels, petroleum jelly.

A. Place a drop of water in the center of the slide with an eyedropper.

B. Use tweezers to place the sample on top of the water drop.

C. Hold the cover slip upright so that one edge of the slip touches the edge of the drop of water.

D. Gently lower the cover slip over the drop of water and sample, trying not to trap any air bubbles.

Making a wet mount. The cover slip is lowered into position over a water drop containing the sample. Top: The drop. Middle: Lowering the cover slip. Bottom: The finished wet mount.

E. Blot up excess water with a tissue or paper towel.

F. If your slide begins to dry out while you are looking at it, place a drop of water next to the cover slip on a side that still seems wet. The water will move under the cover slip and will push out any air bubbles.

G. If you will be viewing a wet mount for a long period of time, use a toothpick to put a thin seal of petroleum jelly around the outside of the cover slip to prevent evaporation.

PULLING A STAIN

Pulling a stain lets you stain a specimen that is already placed on a slide. You will need: stain such as India ink, slide and cover slip, tissue, eyedropper.

A. Prepare a slide using the wet-mount technique.

B. Use an eyedropper to place a drop of stain next to the cover slip.

C. Carefully touch a piece of tissue or paper towel to the side of the cover slip opposite the drop of stain.

D. The drop will move through the sample, and the tissue or towel will become damp.

E. Add more stain, until the stain begins to show on the tissue or paper towel. Carefully blot up any extra stain from the sides of the cover slip.

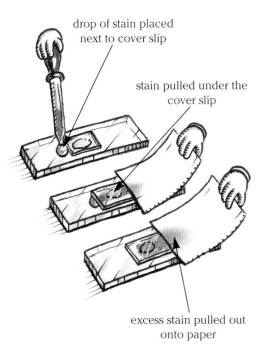

drop of stain placed next to cover slip

stain pulled under the cover slip

excess stain pulled out onto paper

Steps in pulling a stain. Top: The drop of stain is placed next to cover slip. Middle: The stain is pulled under the cover slip. Bottom: The excess stain is pulled out onto the paper towel.

MAKING A WELL SLIDE

A well slide is useful for looking at specimens living in liquids such as pond water. Store-bought ones have a bowl-shaped hollow. You can make one from a regular slide. You will need: clear colorless nail polish; a slide and a cover slip, a toothpick, an eyedropper, and paper towels.

A. Place a slide on a clean paper towel on a flat surface.

B. In the center of the slide, use a toothpick to draw a circle with nail polish about ½ inch (1 cm) in diameter. Allow the nail polish to dry.

C. Add several additional layers to the circle; let the polish dry completely between each layer. This creates a "well" on the slide.

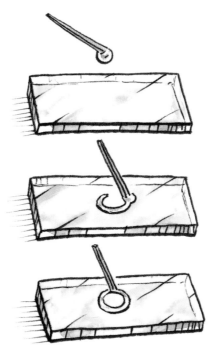

Making a well slide.

MAKING A SMEAR SLIDE

A smear slide is useful for liquid specimens. You will need: two slides and a cover slip, an eyedropper or toothpick, and paper towels.

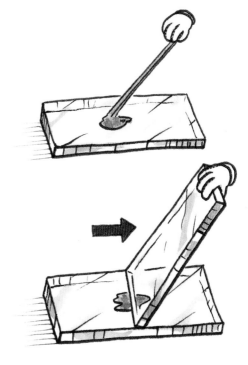

Making a smear slide. Place the specimen on the slide with a toothpick or eyedropper. Smear the specimen with the end of a second slide.

A. Use an eyedropper or toothpick to place a small drop of the sample on one end of a clean slide.

B. Drag the edge of another clean slide across the liquid to spread a thin layer over the top surface of the bottom slide.

C. Gently lower the cover slip over the smear, trying not to trap any air bubbles.

D. Blot up excess liquid with a facial tissue or paper towel.

MAKING A SQUASH SLIDE

This technique can be used with very soft samples. You will need: an eyedropper, a slide and cover slip, lens paper, tweezers, and petroleum jelly.

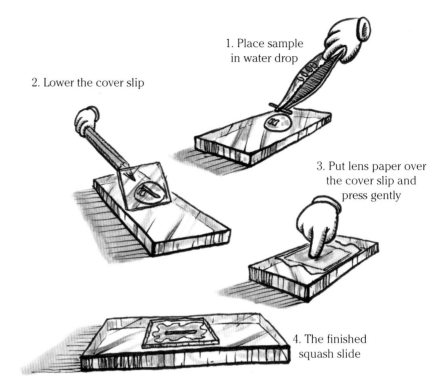

1. Place sample in water drop
2. Lower the cover slip
3. Put lens paper over the cover slip and press gently
4. The finished squash slide

Making a squash slide.

A. Use an eyedropper to place a drop of water in the center of the slide.

B. Place a small piece of the sample on top of the water with a pair of tweezers.

C. Place the cover slip over the sample.

D. Cover the cover slip with a piece of lens paper and press down to gently flatten the sample. Be careful not to break the cover slip.

E. Blot up any excess liquid with the lens paper.

F. If your slide begins to dry out while you are looking at it, place a drop of water next to the cover slip on the side that is the wettest. The water will be pulled under the cover slip.

G. To prevent evaporation, use a toothpick to place a small seal of petroleum jelly around the outside of the cover slip.

ANIMAL INTERIORS

For thousands of years, people have wanted to find out how living things function. Over the centuries, people learned how to grind lenses and look at very small things they couldn't see with their eyes alone. They became explorers of inner space. Modern technology has made it even easier to learn about the inner workings of the body and to help people. MRI (magnetic resonance imaging) can be used to study the brain and other organs. Ultrasound equipment can take a moving picture of your insides, or even of a baby in its mother's womb. Fiber-optic bundles attached to a microscope can be used to look inside the body during microsurgery.

You can start to explore inner space too, using your microscope. Many living things have specialized parts called organs that carry out special jobs. For example, the heart pumps blood, and a fish's gills allow it to get oxygen out of water. Organs are made up of groups of specialized cells called tissues. In this section of the book, we'll learn how to examine some animal tissues.

Chills My Bone Right to the Marrow

If you looked inside a bone, you would see that it has a soft, yellowish substance inside which looks like lard, and also a soft red part. The tissue filling the inner spaces of the bone is called the marrow. The red marrow in the "hollow" center of the large bones of mammals, reptiles, and birds produces new blood cells, including red blood cells, platelets, and some white blood cells. The yellow marrow is used to store fat.

You Will Need

➜ a small bit of marrow from a raw beef or lamb bone

➜ toothpick

➜ slides and cover slips

➜ tincture of iodine

➜ microscope

Note: Make sure to wash your hands and equipment, counters, and utensils with hot, soapy water after you use them. Do not eat raw marrow.

What to Do

1. Get a tiny scrap of bone marrow. The sample doesn't need to be any bigger than the white of your fingernail.

2. Use a toothpick to place the sample and carefully smear the marrow on a slide (see Making a Smear Slide on page 13). Gently lower the cover slip over the sample, trying not to capture any bubbles.

3. Stain the slide with tincture of iodine (see Pulling a Stain on page 12).

4. Observe the slide under the low- and high-power objectives.

What Happened

If you look at yellow marrow, you probably can see large fat cells. These look like large round or oval shapes. If you look at red bone marrow, you may see some red blood cells. There are also a variety of small, dark cells, which are the blood-forming cells of the bone marrow.

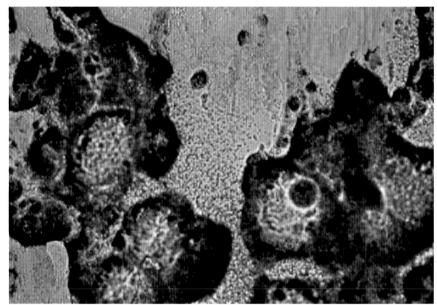
Beef bone marrow at 125✕; enlarged.

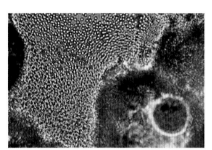
Red blood cells in beef bone marrow at 312.5✕; enlarged.

Red blood cells in beef bone marrow at 312.5✕; enlarged.

ℐCIENCE ℱAIR

Compare the marrow of different animals. How much fat is found in the marrow of a cow's bone compared to that of a lamb? Why does one animal seem to have more marrow in its bones? Fish produce new blood cells in an organ called the spleen. Get a tiny piece of fish spleen at the fish market. Make a slide of spleen and compare this tissue to your bone marrow slides. Find out what the purpose of the spleen is in mammals.

Right at the End of Your Nose ⚠

Rub your nose with your fingers. Now feel all around your ears. You are feeling something called cartilage. Cartilage is a firm, elastic connective tissue found in joints and other places in many animals, including birds, mammals, reptiles, and fish. It helps keeps our bones from grinding together. It also acts as a support. Whales have cartilage at the ends of their bones, and a shark's entire skeleton is made of cartilage. Cartilage is light but strong. It's easy to identify the cartilage on a chicken bone: it is the shiny, smooth white or yellow plastic tissue at the ends. Let's see what cartilage looks like close up.

You Will Need

➜ chicken or turkey cartilage*
➜ knife
➜ tweezers
➜ slide and cover slip
➜ India ink
➜ eyedropper
➜ microscope
➜ microtome

*A small piece, from a leg bone or breastbone, for example.

What to Do

1. Have an adult use a sharp knife to cut a very fine, thin piece of cartilage. The thinner the slice, the better you will be able to see the details with the microscope. Use a microtome if possible (see page 12).

2. Use tweezers to place the sample on a slide. Gently place the cover slip over the sample.

3. Stain your sample with India ink (see Pulling a Stain, page 12).

4. Observe the stained sample using the low- and high-power objectives.

What Happened

There were groups of rounded cells, surrounded by solid material. The rounded cells are chondrocytes, which make the cartilage. They often contain large fat droplets, which you may also be able to see. The chondrocytes use the fat as a food source. The part between the chondrocytes is called the matrix.

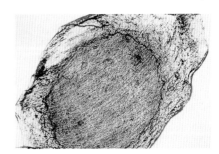

Turkey cartilage at 31.25✕; enlarged.

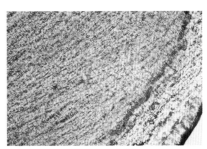

Turkey cartilage at 125✕; enlarged.

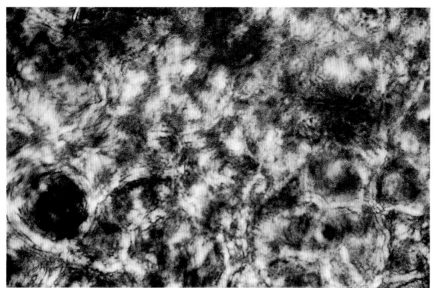

Turkey cartilage at 500×; enlarged.

SCIENCE FAIR

Compare the cartilage of several animals. Does a chicken's resemble a cow's? How does cartilage compare to bone in strength, flexibility, and weight?

Muscle Beef Party

Stand in front of a mirror and flex your arm to make a muscle. Muscles do more than make you look good in your clothes. Skeletal muscles move the bones of your skeleton. Other muscles make the food you eat move through your body. Your heart, which pumps the blood around inside your body, is one big muscle. Just like people, animals have muscles, too. Here is a way to learn about muscles and see what they look like.

Note: Make sure to wash your hands and all equipment, counters, and utensils with hot, soapy water after use. Do not eat raw meat.

You Will Need

➜ a small piece of fresh, uncooked meat, such as beef or turkey

➜ pins or sharp, round tooth-picks

➜ tweezers

➜ tincture of iodine

➜ slide and cover slip

➜ microscope

What to Do

1. Get a tiny, nonfatty piece of raw meat. The sample doesn't need to be any bigger than a dime.

2. Place the meat on a plate and use the pins or toothpicks to gently separate the meat. You should be able to see small lines or fibers.

3. Using the tweezers, place the sample fibers on a slide and gently lower the cover slip over the sample, trying not to capture any bubbles.

4. Stain the slide with tincture of iodine (see Pulling a Stain on page 12).

5. Observe the slide under the low- and high-power objectives.

What Happened

You probably saw some fiber-like structures with fine lines running across them, as in the turkey muscle photo above. You may have seen some darker, round structures. Most of what we think of as meat is skeletal muscle. Skeletal muscle is made up of long fibers with cross stripings or striations. (That's why skeletal muscle is also called striated muscle.) The fibers are made up of threadlike structures called myofibrils. The myofibrils are made of even smaller structures called myofilaments, which are

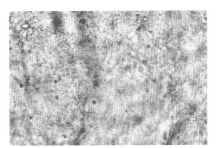
Beef muscle at 500×; enlarged.

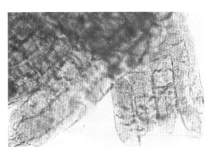
Beef muscle at 125×; enlarged.

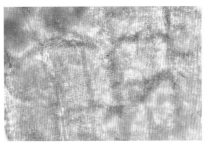
Beef muscle at 312.5×; enlarged.

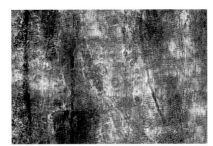
Turkey muscle at 500×, showing striations; enlarged.

made of protein. The dark round structures are the cells' nuclei, the control centers of the muscle cells. The muscle fibers contract to shorten the muscle, to make parts of your body move. When a muscle contracts, the myofilaments slide along each other.

SCIENCE FAIR

In addition to skeletal muscle, there are two other types of muscle: cardiac (heart) muscle and smooth (visceral) muscle. Smooth muscle is found in the lining of the blood vessels and in organs. Get a small piece of cow or chicken heart. Make slides and compare them to your skeletal muscle slides. Take a small piece of a blood vessel (a vein or artery) from a chicken leg and compare this as well.

Compare the muscle fibers in a piece of beef to those in a piece of a chicken. What differences are there?

Tiny Warriors

Have you ever cut or stuck yourself with something sharp? Your cut probably bled a bit and then stopped bleeding. Why didn't you just keep on bleeding? Several kinds of blood cells at the place of your injury rushed to the scene and started repair work. Here's a chance to have a close look at some of the brave fighters that keep you healthy.

Experimenting with human blood is not a good idea, because it can transmit diseases such as hepatitis and AIDS. A safer way to examine blood is to use the blood from a chicken or cow.

Note: Make sure to wash your hands and all equipment, counters, and utensils with hot, soapy water after use. Do not eat raw meat.

You Will Need

→ tiny piece of raw beef or chicken liver

→ tweezers

→ three slides and 2 cover slips

→ eyedropper

→ India ink

→ microscope

What to Do

1. Get a tiny piece of raw beef or chicken liver. The sample doesn't need to be any bigger than the white of your fingernail.

2. Use the tweezers to squeeze a drop of blood from the liver onto the slide.

3. Make a smear slide (see page 13 for directions). Spread the blood out very thin across the slide so it appears to be yellow, not red. Allow the blood to dry. Gently lower the cover slip over the smear, trying not to trap any bubbles.

4. Examine your slide under the low- and high-power objectives.

5. Make another slide using the same technique, but this time, when the blood has dried, add a tiny drop of India ink to stain the slide. Place a cover slip over the slide and view it under the microscope. Does it look any different than the first slide?

What Happened

You saw the cells that are part of blood. The blood sample was exposed to the air, so it may have begun to clump together, or clot. Clotting happens when blood encounters a rough surface, or even glass. Blood consists of a straw-colored fluid called plasma, in which millions of blood cells and platelets are suspended. You may have seen red blood cells (erythrocytes), which are disk-shaped. They carry oxygen

Beef blood from liver at 500✕; enlarged.

from the lungs to all the parts of the body and return carbon dioxide to be exhaled. You may have seen white blood cells (leukocytes). Leukocytes are larger than red blood cells. There are several kinds. White blood cells may appear round or irregularly shaped. They fight infections and destroy bacteria. You may have seen some platelets—small, irregularly shaped cell fragments. Proteins in the platelets start a reaction that forms a mass or clot when

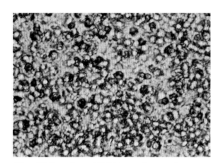

Beef blood at 500×; enlarged.

there is an injury. In your body, clotting stops too much blood from flowing out when you cut yourself.

SCIENCE FAIR

There are some differences between the blood cells of mammals like cows, pigs and sheep and those of birds such as chickens, ducks, and turkeys. Make slides using blood from these animals and compare them. Why do you think there are differences?

Fish Noses ⚠

Fish have nostrils, but they don't use them for breathing. Instead, they use them for taste and smell. For breathing, fish have gills. Clams, oysters, scallops, and other members of the group of shellfish called bivalves also have gills. Clams use their gills for breathing and for eating; some even temporarily store their eggs there. Let's find out how gills work.

You Will Need

➜ fresh clam
➜ sharp knife
➜ tweezers
➜ slide
➜ cover slip
➜ microscope

What to Do

1. Have an adult open the clam if necessary and use a sharp knife to remove the gills from the clam (see photograph on page 22).

2. Use tweezers to gently place small pieces of the gills on the slide and squash (see Making a Squash Slide on page 14).

Cover the sample with a cover slip, being careful not to trap any air bubbles.

3. View the slide using the low- and high-power objectives.

Note: Make sure to wash your hands and all equipment, counters, and utensils with hot, soapy water after use.

What Happened

Clam gills look feathery. This is because they are made up of cells that have tiny fingerlike cilia sticking out of them. Cilia are fine, movable, hairlike structures on the surface of the gills. The cilia circulate the water around the gills and give the cells a large surface area, so it is easy for oxygen from the water to enter the blood vessels in the gills and for carbon dioxide to pass out of the gills. Our own lungs have cilia on their inside surface for just the same reason (except that they get oxygen from air). Clams also use their cilia to trap food and direct it into their mouths. Clams and other bivalves are filter feeders. This means that they extract food from the water that runs through their gills. The cilia in the clam's gills are a little bit slimy, because they are coated in mucus. The food sticks to the mucus when the water is expelled by the clam.

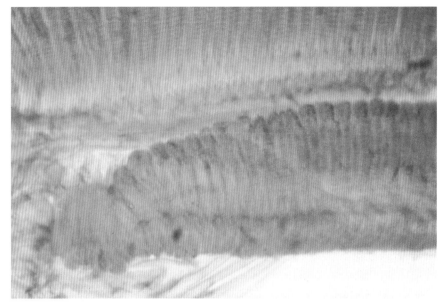
Clam gills at 60×; enlarged.

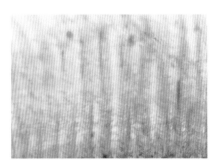
Sardine gills at 250×.

Clam, showing location of gills.

Science Fair

Compare and contrast the slides of clam gills with prepared slides of fish gills or of lung tissue from another animal. Draw or photograph your slides to show the differences and similarities. Make slides of gill tissue from other bivalves, such as oysters or scallops. What do they have in common with each other? How are they different from the fish gills? Are the gills of fish that are found deeper in the ocean different from those of fish found nearer the surface?

Bathing Beauties ⚠

Did you know that sponges are actually animals? They don't bark or roll over, and they aren't playful. They're very simple compared to the other animals we've looked at. There are over 5000 kinds of sponges. Some are bath sponges, which make terrific bathing companions. They feel good on your skin and they'll get you really clean. Many sponges people use around the house now are not real sponges, but synthetic (artificial) substitutes. Let's look at the difference between synthetic and natural sponges.

You Will Need

→ scissors

→ natural sponge*

→ craft knife, single-sided razor blade, or microtome

→ synthetic sponge

→ slide

→ water

→ cover slip

→ household bleach

→ eyedropper

→ microscope

→ paper towel

*Look for sponges at a hardware store, drug store, pottery supply store, etc.

What to Do

1. Have an adult cut a small slice of natural sponge that is thinner than a sheet of paper. Use a microtome to do this if you wish (see page 12).

2. Make a wet mount of the natural sponge, flattening the piece in a drop of water (see instructions for making a wet mount, page 12).

3. Examine your slide under the microscope, using both the low-power and high-power objectives.

4. Remove the cover slip and add a drop of bleach. Replace the cover slip and blot around the slide carefully with a piece of paper towel to remove any extra bleach.

5. Examine your slide under the microscope, using both the low-power and high-power objectives.

6. Cut a small slice of synthetic sponge that is thinner than a sheet of paper.

7. Make a wet mount of the synthetic sponge, flattening the slice in a drop of water.

8. Examine your second slide, using both the low- and high-power objectives. Compare the synthetic sponge to the natural sponge.

What Happened

The natural sponge is made up of several different kinds of cells. The cells are held together by proteins. When you added the bleach, the protein dissolved and you could see the other cells more clearly. The larger cells are called collar cells or choanocytes. Collar cells have hairlike flagella that move the water through the sponge. The collar cells trap food particles. Depending on the kind of sponge, you may have seen crystal-shaped structures (spicules).

Natural sponges are filter feeders. They live at the bottom of the ocean or in freshwater, attached to rocks or other things. They filter water through their bodies through their pores to get their food. The food gets trapped in the rough areas that line the collar cells, and the sponges digest it.

The synthetic sponge wasn't made of cells. It was made of a manufactured material with air spaces in it, which act like the spaces in the natural sponge.

SCIENCE FAIR

Get another natural sponge, such as an elephant's ear sponge, used by potters, or the kind used to wash cars. (If you go to the seashore, you may find a sponge attached to a clam shell.) Repeat steps 1 through 5 of the experiment and compare your results.

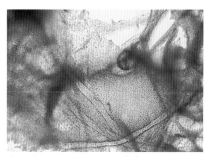

Synthetic sponge at 60✕; enlarged.

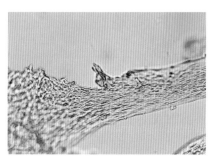

Synthetic sponge at 250✕; enlarged.

Synthetic sponge at 125✕; enlarged.

Synthetic sponge at 500✕; enlarged.

Natural sponge at 31.25✕; enlarged.

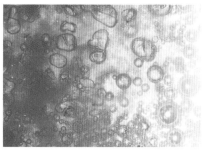

Natural sponge showing spicules at 500✕; enlarged.

Natural sponge after adding bleach at 125✕; enlarged.

Bleach attacking natural sponge at 31.25✕; enlarged.

BACTERIA

Among the very simplest living things on earth are the bacteria. These creatures were probably the earliest living things. Each tiny bacterial cell has a cell wall, a cell membrane, cytoplasm containing a chromosome, and other structures that help it live. Bacteria are classified by their shapes. Rod-shaped bacteria are called bacilli. Bacteria that are small spheres clumped together like bunches of grapes are called cocci. Corkscrew-shaped bacteria are called spirilla. Some bacteria live together in strings or clumps, and some have tiny, whiplike flagella which allow them to move around. In addition to living in air, water, and soil, bacteria live on other living things, such as plants or animals. In fact, millions of them live in and on your body right now.

While many kinds of bacteria can harm you, there are some kinds that help you. Some even work to create foods and drinks. The yogurt in your fridge and the sauerkraut on your plate are the products of bacteria. Wine and beer also are made by the action of bacteria. Some bacteria, however, like the bacteria growing in your mouth, aren't particularly good for you or your teeth. Other bacteria, like Escherichia coli, which can cause intestinal infections, can be harmful and even deadly. Studying bacteria helps scientists and doctors to diagnose, treat, and eventually cure some diseases.

Active Culture

Many yogurts that you can buy in grocery stores contain an "active culture." This means that the yogurt contains live yogurt bacteria. Unlike harmful bacteria, which cause disease, these bacteria simply change milk into yogurt.

Note: Make sure to wash your hands and all equipment, counters, and utensils after use. Do not eat the sample you use on the slide.

You Will Need

→ a container of plain yogurt with a live culture

→ toothpick

→ slide and cover slip

→ eyedropper

→ water

→ tissue

What to Do

1. Use a toothpick to take a small sample of yogurt from the container. Smear this on a slide. (See Making a Smear Slide on page 13.)

2. Place a small drop of water on the sample to thin out the yogurt.

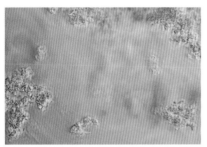

Yogurt at 500×; enlarged.

3. Place the cover slip over the sample, trying not to trap any bubbles. Blot up any excess with a tissue.

4. Observe the slide using the low- and high-power objectives.

What Happened

There were tiny rod-shaped or round live bacteria slowly moving around in the sample. You probably saw them moving in between the large clumps of yogurt.

When they are placed in fresh milk and kept warm (about 110°F or 44°C), the yogurt bacteria will turn the milk into yogurt.

SCIENCE FAIR

Get several other brands of yogurt. Make slides and compare them to your original ones. Do the different brands of yogurt have the same kind of bacteria? Keeping the magnification the same for all the slides, estimate the number of bacteria you see. Try storing the yogurt at room temperature for several days. Does the number of bacteria in the sample increase?

Sweet and Sour

*Yogurt isn't the only food that is created by bacteria. Sauerkraut, made from shredded cabbage, also is formed by the action of bacteria. Unlike yogurt, which usually is made by adding bacteria to milk, sauerkraut is made by placing shredded cabbage in a crock with salt and spices and letting its own natural bacteria take over to **ferment** the cabbage. Let's compare the bacteria found in yogurt to those found in sauerkraut.*

You Will Need

→ fresh sauerkraut (not canned)

→ slide and cover slip

→ eyedropper

→ microscope

→ tissue

What to Do

1. Place a drop of sauerkraut liquid on a slide and gently lower a cover slip over the sample. Blot up any excess liquid with a tissue.

2. View the sample under the low- and high-power objectives.

What Happened

The bacteria that make sauerkraut are similar to those that make yogurt. There are three different types of bacteria in sauerkraut. You may have been able to see one or more kinds. They use the sugar present in the cabbage to make lactic acid, which gives sauerkraut its sour taste.

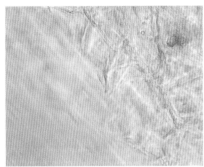

Sauerkraut at 500✕; enlarged.

SCIENCE FAIR

Compare different brands of canned sauerkraut to fresh sauerkraut. What differences did you see? Why do you think they don't look the same?

Toothpicks

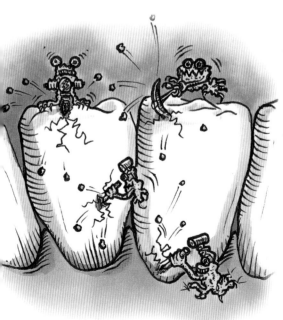

When you wake up in the morning, do your teeth ever feel slimy? To give you an idea of what's happening in your mouth, here's an experiment that is guaranteed to encourage you to take extra care with your dental hygiene.

You Will Need

➜ toothpick

➜ 2 slides and cover slips

➜ spoon

➜ food coloring

➜ microscope

What to Do

1. Use a toothpick to gently scrape between your teeth or around your gums to get a sample of the stuff that's there.

2. Smear the sample on the toothpick onto a slide (see instructions for making a smear slide on page 13).

3. Gather a drop of saliva on a spoon and drop it onto your sample. Place the cover slip over the sample, trying not to trap any bubbles.

4. View the sample under the low- and high-power objectives. What did you see?

5. Try this experiment again, this time using food coloring instead of saliva.

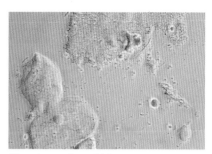
Mouth swab at 500×.

What Happened

You may have seen small pieces of food or bubbles from your saliva, and you probably saw some tiny bacteria. The yellowish white material you got from between your teeth is called plaque. It forms on your teeth when you don't brush them. Bacteria grow in the plaque. The bacteria start making acids out of leftover food. The acids can eat away at the enamel on your teeth, causing cavities. The sample with the food coloring was easier to see than the sample with the saliva, because the coloring stained the bacteria and food particles.

SCIENCE FAIR

The bacteria that live in plaque eat carbohydrates. See the effect candy, toothpaste, and mouthwash have on the bacteria in your mouth. Do the Toothpicks experiment several times: once after eating candy without brushing your teeth and once after brushing; once after eating candy and using mouthwash. Which sample had the most bacteria?

Four-Leaf Clover

Some people try to get rid of clover in their lawns. They think the clover ruins the grass. Instead of trying to kill this plant, people should try to grow even more of it! Clover is actually good for soil and plants. To learn more about clover and similar plants, find yourself a patch of clover and read on.

You Will Need

→ roots of a clover plant
→ water
→ tissue
→ needle or pin
→ slide
→ cover slip
→ eyedropper
→ microscope

What to Do

1. Pull or dig up a clover plant from a garden or lawn. Try to find one with whitish nodules (little bumps) on the roots.

2. Rinse the plant off in water to remove any dirt from the roots; then dry it with a paper towel.

3. Pluck off a large whitish nodule and place it on the center of a slide.

4. Prick the nodule with a needle or pin. Squash the nodule and rub it around on the center of the slide so that liquid from the nodule is spread around the slide.

5. Place a drop of water on the slide, using the eyedropper.

6. Gently lower the cover slip over the smear, trying not to trap any air bubbles.

7. Blot up excess liquid with a tissue or paper towel.

8. Place the slide on the stage of the microscope and secure it with the stage clips. Observe your slide using the low- and high-power objectives.

What Happened

Using the high-power objective, you probably saw very tiny rod-shaped bacteria. Clover is a nat-ural fertilizer: the *Rhizobium* bacteria living in the nodules on the clover roots take some of the nitrogen gas from the air and turn it into nitrogen compounds, which plants need in order to grow. These bacteria are called nitrogen-fixing bacteria because they capture nitrogen from the air. The bacteria use the roots of the plant for food and protection. This help-

Bacteria from a clover root nodule at 400×; enlarged.

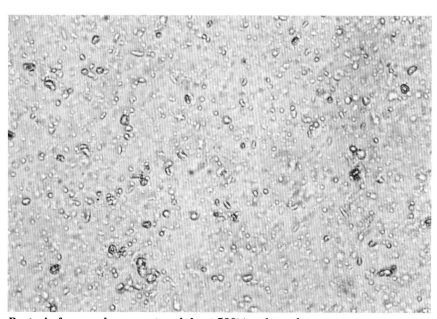
Bacteria from a clover root nodule at 500×; enlarged.

ing relationship between two different types of living things that are found living closely together is called symbiosis.

SCIENCE FAIR

Compare the clover nodule bacteria to those found in yogurt, sauerkraut, or even ones found in your mouth. Look at some bacteria from the roots of another legume, such as a garden pea. Draw pictures of each to show their similarities and differences.

CREEPY, CRAWLY, SNEEZY STUFF

If you own a pet, you know that your pet sheds its fur or loses its skin or feathers at certain times of the year. Snakes shed their skin, birds moult, and dogs may shed some of their heavier winter coats during the spring.

But did you know that people also shed their skins? Flakes of dead skin fall off our bodies each day. These bits are so small that you probably don't notice them. All these things can then become food for micro-scopic creatures such as house mites. This section will examine some living creatures. It will help you understand why some pets feel softer to cuddle than others. We'll also look at some pollen.

Dust Bunnies*

Just below your bed, hiding in your carpet or balled up in a corner of the floor, are micro-scopic samples just waiting to be found. Lurking in the mound of dust are hairs, dead skin, and tiny bugs called house mites. It wouldn't matter if you vacu-umed your room every day, you'd never be able to rid your home of the billions of these creatures hiding in every space. Mites are so tiny that, even with your microscope, you might have difficulty identifying them. It's worth a try.

*Sneeze alert: Be careful handling dust if you are allergic to house dust.

You Will Need

→ small bits of dust**
→ envelope
→ pencil
→ slide
→ tweezers
→ microscope

**Get dust from different areas of the house: under the bed, beneath the cush-ions in your couch, etc.

What to Do

1. Gather small bits of dust from different areas around your house. Place each sample

A house mite *(Glyciphagus domesticus)*, enlarged about 100×.

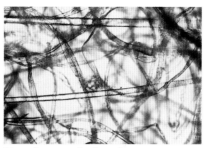

Dust from a clothes dryer at 31.25×; enlarged.

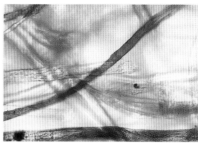

Dust from a clothes dryer at 125×; enlarged.

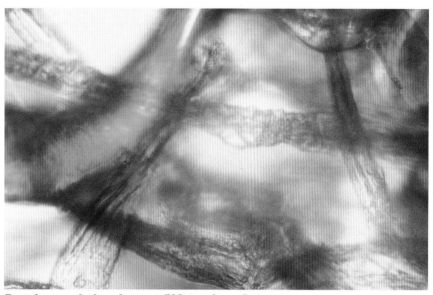

Dust from a clothes dryer at 500×; enlarged.

in an envelope and label the envelope showing the area you collected it from.

2. Use the tweezers to take a tiny amount of the sample and place it on a slide. Cover it with a cover slip.

3. View the slide using the low- and high-power objectives. Could you find anything that was moving? Did you see any thick cylinders? They might be hairs. (See the Fur Coats experiment for more about hairs.)

4. Observe the other samples you collected. Did they all look the same under the microscope?

What Happened

There were all sorts of interesting things that you could see from the samples. There may have been bits and pieces of insect wings and legs, thread, bread crumbs, and even flaked skin. This is dinner for house mites. Perhaps you were even able to find a house mite. Mites are tiny creatures that are related to spiders (see illustration). House mites don't bite and they don't usually cause problems unless you are allergic to them.

SCIENCE FAIR

Make slides and compare the dust samples from different areas of your house. Do you see more mites in areas that are used more often? Compare a sample from under your bed to a sample from a storage area such as the back of a closet.

Fur Coats

When you pet a cat does the fur feel softer than a dog's coat? Do you think a bunny's coat would feel even softer than a cat's? When viewed under a microscope, you will be able to see the differences between the fur or hair of different animals.

You Will Need

→ a few hairs from several animals such as a cat, dog, rabbit, hamster

→ slide and cover slip

→ eyedropper

→ tweezers

→ water

→ microscope

→ pencil and labels

→ paper towels

→ toothpick and petroleum jelly

What to Do

1. Brush your pet gently to remove a few hairs. Cut a piece of hair about ½ inch (1 cm) in length, and make a wet mount of the hair piece. (See instructions for making a wet mount on page 12.)

2. Place the slide on the stage of the microscope and secure it with the stage clips. Observe your slide using the low-power and high-power objectives. Record your observations.

3. Make more slides using the hair or fur from other pets. Make a slide of your own hair.

4. Observe these slides using the low-power and high-power objectives. Compare the different hair samples. Record your observations.

What Happened

Some dogs, like poodles, have hair that is quite curly. Other breeds of dogs, like Dalmatians, have short straight hair. Cat hair is usually finer than dog hair, but thicker than rabbit hair. Human hair varies in thickness, but is usually thicker than the hair of cats or rabbits. Animals' hair serves a useful purpose. Some sea mammals, like otters, have water-resistant, short, stiff hair and soft under-fur, which protects them from the cold water. Polar bears have whitish fur that is water repellent and camouflages the bears against the snow and ice. The hair of a sheep (fleece) is thick, fluffy and oily, while the fur of a rabbit is smooth and very fine.

Dog hair at 250X; enlarged.

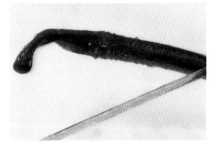

Human hair from head (thin); from beard (thick), at 500X; enlarged.

Human hair at 125X; enlarged.

Guinea pig hair at 125X; enlarged.

Guinea pig hair at 312.5X; enlarged.

Guinea pig hair at 500X; enlarged.

science fair

Compare the fur of different animals and explain how that kind of fur helps the animal. Do animals that normally live in hot climates have different kinds of hair from those that live in colder regions? Visit your local zoo or pet store and ask the zookeeper to give you samples of fur from different animals. Make slides with the different hair samples and look at them under the microscope. Draw pictures of the hair fibers and measure their thickness. Do the hairs have any unusual features?

Flower Power*

There's an old saying that goes, *"Stop and smell the flowers every day."* We feel that not only should you stop and smell the flowers, you should also stop and study the flowers, too. Flowers are not only beautiful and fragrant, but also interesting. In this experiment, you'll learn something of how flowers work and you will "trick" some pollen into germinating.

Part One

MAKE A POLLEN SLIDE

You Will Need

→ pollen from several kinds of flowers**

→ slides

→ cover slips

→ water

→ eyedropper

→ microscope

→ labels

→ pen and paper

*Sneeze alert: Do not perform this experiment if you are allergic to pollen.

**Look for flowers that have lots of powdery pollen on the anthers, like lilies and petunias, as these will give you the best results. See the flower diagram to learn where the anthers are.

What to Do

1. Pull a stamen off the flower. Hold the stamen above the center of the slide and shake the stamen so that some of the pollen falls off onto the slide. (If the pollen is really sticky, try blowing lightly on the anther to loosen the pollen.)

2. Use the eyedropper to place a drop or two of plain water onto the center of the slide. Make a wet mount following the directions on page 12. Label the slide with the pollen source.

3. Place the slide on the stage of the microscope and secure it with the stage clips. Observe your slide under low and high power.

4. Repeat steps 1 through 3 for each kind of flower you have.

Part Two

GROW A POLLEN TUBE

Now that you know what pollen looks like, you can grow a pollen tube.

You Will Need

→ sugar

→ measuring cup

→ teaspoon

→ eyedropper

→ pollen

→ slides and cover slips

→ warm water

→ pen and paper

What to Do

1. Place 1 teaspoon (5 mL) of sugar in 1 cup (250 mL) of lukewarm water. Stir the water to dissolve the sugar.

2. Sprinkle pollen onto a slide as you did in Part One. Use the eyedropper to add a drop of sugar water to the slide, and make a wet mount. Note the kind of pollen used and the amount of sugar in the water you used.

3. Immediately place the slide under a lamp or in a very warm spot in the house. Watch the slide closely.

4. After about 10 minutes, place the slide on the stage of the microscope and secure it with the stage clips. Observe your slide under low and high power. Record your results. If nothing has happened, put the slide back in a warm spot again.

5. Check on the slide every 10 minutes or so. If nothing has happened after about 90 minutes, take some new pollen and add more sugar to the sugar-water mixture.

6. For each attempt, keep a record of the kind of pollen, the amount of sugar in the mixture, and the amount of time it took for something to happen.

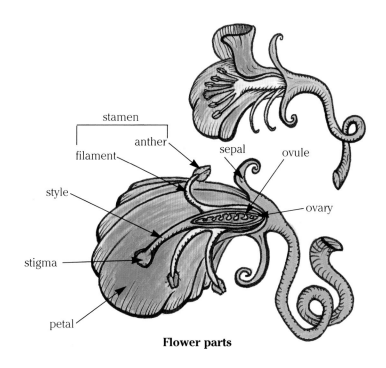

Flower parts

What Happened

Part One: You saw pollen grains. Depending on the flowers you chose, the grains may have been squarish, round, or star-shaped, or another shape. Each kind of plant has its own unique pollen grains.

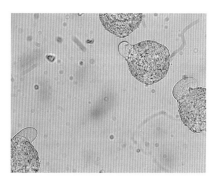

Pollen tube at 400✕; enlarged.

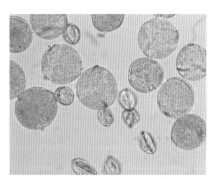

Pollen from a petunia at 400✕; enlarged.

Part Two: When you added sugar water to the pollen grains and heated them, you tricked the pollen into germinating, or starting to grow. Pollen grains contain the male cells of the flowering plant. Their "job" is to meet up with a female cell or ovule of a plant, and join together to form a seed. From the seed a new plant can grow. The top (the stigma) of the female organ of the flower has a sugary coating. Pollen grains, carried by insects or the wind, or some other way, stick to the coating and start to germinate.

When a pollen grain starts to germinate, it gets larger. Then the pollen grain grows a pollen tube. In a plant, this tube works its way down through the style of the flower to the ovary, where the ovules are (see diagram on page 35).

The sugar you added to the water acts like the coating on the stigma of the flower. The amount of sugar that will cause pollen to start germinating varies, depending on the type of flower you used.

SCIENCE FAIR

Are certain kinds of pollen easier to work with than others? How does the mixture of the solution affect the experiment? Does temperature play a part in the creation of pollen tubes? Try a sample at room temperature, another in a warm window, and another in the refrigerator to find out. Look at your samples under the microscope and record the results.

PLANTS

Studying plants is an exciting way to discover how living things work. Plants are all around us, and samples are easy to *get. The lowly dandelion or the prickly burr can teach you about how new plants get started, while onions from your fridge* *can help you learn how nutrients move in and out of plants. You can even find some surprising things in a handful of beans.*

Jack and the Beanstalk ⚠

Poor Jack! He traded his cow for a handful of what his mother thought were useless beans. Lo and behold! A bean grew into a plant that stretched up to the sky. What do you think goes on inside a bean plant like that? You can't get the same kind of beans Jack had, but using your microscope, you can find out what happens inside a bean plant.

You Will Need

➜ bean seeds from a nursery or plant store

➜ paper toweling

➜ water

➜ clear plastic container with lid

➜ clear plastic lid or petri dish

➜ eyedropper

➜ India ink

➜ microscope

➜ knife

➜ book

What to Do

1. Soak the beans in cold water for 12 hours. Dampen a paper towel with water and place it in the bottom of a plastic container. Put several beans on the toweling and put the lid on the container. Put the container in a warm, dark spot for several days.

2. When the beans have sprouted roots, open the container to allow the leaves of the plant to grow above the edge of the container. Make sure you keep the paper towel damp. Put the container in a light place. Let the sprouts continue to grow. Do the following experiment after each sprout has several large leaves.

3. Place a clear plastic lid or petri dish on the microscope stage. Fill this with 2 to 3 tablespoons (30 to 45 mL) of water and add 2 drops of India ink to the water.

4. Cut the bean plant stem off just above the seed. Immediately place the cut stem in the lid containing water and India ink. Support the rest of the bean plant by resting it on a book.

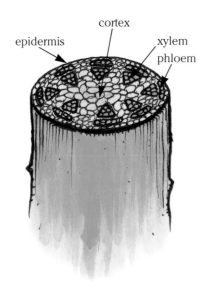

cortex

epidermis

xylem

phloem

Cross-section of stem.

5. Use the low-power objective to look at the stem near where it comes out of the water. Can you see the ink entering the stem? If this is difficult to see, have an adult cut a thin slice off of the upper surface of the stem so that you can view the tubelike cells inside.

What Happened

The India ink let you to see that water was entering the bottom of the stem. Water goes from roots, up the stem, to the leaves of plants through a special tissue called xylem, made up of long, narrow cells. They carry water and nutrients up into the

plant from the roots. The xylem cells are arranged in lines up the stem to act like drinking straws for the plant. India ink contains little particles of carbon, which were transported towards the leaves along with the water, so you were able to see the tubes of xylem cells because the ink colored them.

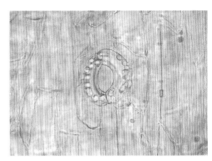

Longitudinal section of bean shoot stem at 500×; enlarged.

Bean shoot stem, showing hairs, at 500×; enlarged.

$\mathcal{S}$CIENCE $\mathcal{F}$AIR

Using your microtome, make cross-sections of the stems of several kinds of plants, including a water plant from an aquarium or pond, a succulent or cactus, and a lily or tulip (monocot). Stain the sections with India ink and look at them under the microscope. Use a camera attached to the microscope or make drawings to record the differences and similarities among the stems of the various plants. Look in a reference book and label the stem parts you can recognize. How did the plants adapt to their special environments?

Beyond Beleaf

If you look around you, you will probably see so many kinds of leaves that's it's hard to believe. Leaves are actually working hard every day, luckily for us. They take in carbon dioxide and, with water taken up by the plant's roots, they make food and oxygen, without which we couldn't live. So, take a deep breath and thank a plant! Let's take a closer look at some leaves and see what we can learn about them.

You Will Need

➜ scissors

➜ young bean leaf*

➜ blade of grass, or leaf from corn, tulip, iris, or bamboo plant

➜ slides

➜ water

➜ cover slips

➜ microscope

*From previous experiment.

What to Do

1. Cut a ½ inch (1 cm) square from the bean leaf.

2. Make a wet mount of the bean leaf (see Making a Wet Mount, page 12).

3. Examine your slide under the microscope, using both the low-power and high-power objectives.

4. Cut a ½ inch (1 cm) square from the corn leaf. Make a wet mount of the corn leaf sample and examine it, as you did with the bean leaf.

5. Compare the corn leaf to the bean leaf.

Monocots and Dicots

When your bean sprouted in Jack and the Beanstalk, you probably noticed that each bean grew two leaves as its first set of leaves (seed leaves). Maybe you never realized it, but all flowering plants start out either like the bean, with two seed leaves, or with only one seed leaf, like corn and iris. Plants with two seed leaves are called dicotyledons (*di* means "two" and *cotyledon* means "seed leaf"). We call them "dicots" for short. Dicots have weblike or spreading veins. Oak trees, roses, and beans are only a few examples of dicots. Plants with one seed leaf are called monocotyledons, or "monocots" for short. (*Mono* means "one.") Corn, grasses, and bamboo are monocots. Each group contains many thousands of different species of plants.

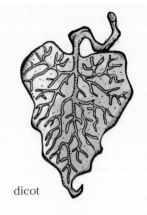

dicot

monocot

What Happened

Both of the leaves were green, but the structure of the bean leaf was quite different from that of the corn leaf. The bean leaf had netlike veins that spread out across the leaf. The corn leaf had parallel veins that ran the length of the leaf. The veins are continuations of the vascular tissues that transport water and nutrients in the plant. Both leaves are green because they have chlorophyll in them, a compound that helps to trap energy from light.

Grass blade at 31.25X; enlarged.

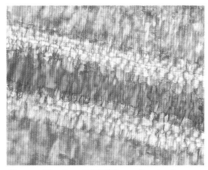

Grass blade at 125X; enlarged.

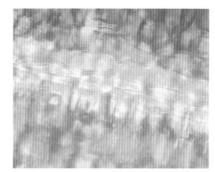

Grass blade at 312.5X; enlarged.

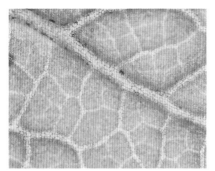

Bean leaf at 31.25X; enlarged.

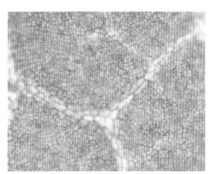

Bean leaf at 312.5X; enlarged.

Bean leaf at 500X; enlarged.

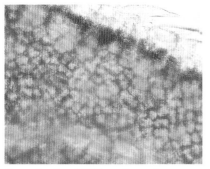

Bean leaf at 125X; enlarged.

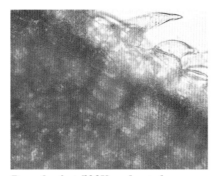

Bean leaf at 500X; enlarged.

SCIENCE FAIR

Look at the leaves of other dicots, such as roses, geraniums, peas, and maple or oak trees, using your microscope. Can you detect any microscopic differences among them? Make drawings to record your findings. Look at leaf samples from other monocots, such as lilies, orchids, palms, or grasses. Can you create a key to tell the different plants apart?

Hooked on Socks

Have you ever gone for a walk in a field or forest, only to find that sharp, sticky burrs or seeds have embedded themselves on your socks and clothes? These stowaways have hitched a ride on you. This is nature's way of scattering them to a fertile new home. When you study burrs, you can begin to see why they can attach themselves to just about anything.

You Will Need*

→ large pair of wooly or fuzzy socks

→ tweezers

→ slide

→ microscope

→ pencil and notebook

→ lamp

→ paper toweling

*If you are walking in the woods, you may also need a compass, buddy, and water. See Tips on page 43.

What to Do

1. Put on an extra-large pair of woolen socks and pull them high up over the bottoms of your pants, so they will brush against nearby plants on your walk. Then put your shoes on. Take a walk through the woods or a field. If you have a pet dog, you might also want to take your pet with you to help collect samples.

2. When you get home, check your socks for sharp burrs or thistles. Give your pet a brushing to see what has become attached to its fur.

3. Use the tweezers to remove any burrs or seeds you have found.

4. Place the burrs or seeds on a slide, shine a light from above, and view them under the low-power objective. (You don't need a cover slip.) Draw a picture of what you see, or write down your findings in words.

5. If you want to know what kinds of seeds you attracted, wrap the seeds in a wet paper towel and put them in a plastic bag until they germinate. Then plant them indoors in earth in a flowerpot. When your plants grow, try to identify them in a field guide.

What Happened

Your socks and your pet's fur attracted various seeds and burrs. A burr is actually the dried ovary (seed pod) of a plant such as a burr chervil. Burrs have hooklike parts that can become attached to anything that touches them, such as the material of your socks. They also can attach themselves to any furry animal that brushes against them. Eventually the burr will drop off or be rubbed off, and the seeds it encloses will land in a new location. If conditions are right (rich earth, water, the right temperature), the seeds inside the burr will be able to grow in their new location into new plants.

Horse chestnut seed casing at 60×; enlarged.

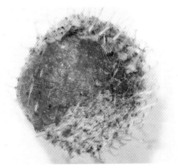

Burr at 120×; enlarged.

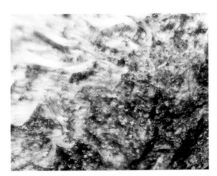

Burr at 500×; enlarged.

SCIENCE FAIR

Many things we see in nature have been sources of ideas for inventions. The simple burr was the inspiration for the hook-and-loop fastener called Velcro, found on ski clothes, bookbags and in other places. Velcro was invented by George DeMestral after he went walking in the woods in Switzerland. Burrs stuck to his clothing. He examined the burrs and got the idea of trying to make a material that would stick to things in the same way they do.

Project 1. Look around you at the different ways that animals and plants live. Try to design a device that will do something usual in an unusual way. Maybe you could design a better type of camouflage cloth by looking at local animal coloration, or a different type of nutcracker by looking at birds' beaks. The possibilities are endless. Be sure to describe how you got the idea and show how it makes the animal or plant more effective in its environment.

Project 2. Examine the seeds of plants in your neighborhood, on their plants and also under the microscope. Try to find out how the seeds are spread around and what conditions they need to grow. How are the seeds of trees spread around?

Some Tips on Walking in the Woods

❧ Get permission from your parents or other adults

❧ Leave word where/when you are going and when you expect to return

❧ Know your destination

❧ Wear the right clothes for your area

❧ Take water and a whistle

❧ Walk with friends

❧ Wear strong shoes

❧ Keep track of your direction (take a compass)

❧ Leave time to return before dark

Pickled Onions

If you have a vegetable in your fridge for a long time, it gets wilted and soft. You can make the vegetable firmer by placing it in ice water. Here is a way of examining how water moves into and out of plant cells.

You Will Need

→ raw purple onion

→ knife and tweezers

→ eyedropper and water

→ slides and cover slips

→ tissue or paper towel

→ salt and spoon

→ microscope

What to Do

1. Slice the raw onion and cut one of the onion rings into ¼ inch (6 mm) sections.

2. Remove the thin skin from the outer, convex side of the onion section by pulling it gently with tweezers.

3. Make a wet mount of the onion skin in a drop of water (see Making a Wet Mount, page 12).

4. Examine your slide under the microscope, using both the low-power and high-power objectives.

5. Dissolve several grains of salt in a spoonful of warm water. Keep adding salt grains until the salt will no longer dissolve and a few grains are left sitting in the salt water. Set it aside.

6. Make a wet mount of a second section of onion skin in plain water. Add the salt water from Step 5 as you would pull a stain (see Pulling a Stain on page 12).

7. Examine your slide using both low and high power objectives. Compare this slide to the one you made using freshwater.

Cell Membranes and Osmosis

The membrane surrounding the contents of a living cell is so thin that you can't see it with a light microscope. This membrane lets certain things into and out of the cell, like water and nutrients the cell needs. We call this kind of membrane selectively permeable (or semi-permeable), which means that it only allows some things to pass through it. Most materials are too large to pass through the membrane, or else they pass through the membrane much more slowly than the tiny water molecules, which can pass through freely.

The passage of water through a selectively permeable membrane is called osmosis. Osmosis occurs because water moves through a membrane to wherever there are more dissolved particles such as salt and sugar, whether that is inside or outside the cells. In our experiment, the dissolved particles were not able to move out through the onion skin membrane, because the structure of the membrane holds them in, so the cells swelled up as water moved in or shriveled as water moved out.

What Happened

In the onion skin in plain water, you saw the long, narrow onion skin cells. You saw the cell walls, which are the nonliving support for the cells. Although you can't see them with a light microscope because they are so thin, the cell membranes were right up against the cell walls in the sample in plain water. The cells looked red throughout because of the red pigment in the onion, anthocyanin, in the cytoplasm (the fluid contents of the cell).

The red onion skin sample in salt water had a different appearance. There were clear areas and distinct reddish areas in the cells. The reddish areas are the shrunken cytoplasm. Because the salt content in the water outside the cells was higher than the salt content inside the cells, some of the water in the cytoplasm moved out of the cells by osmosis. The cell membranes shrank away from the cell walls, leaving empty clear spaces.

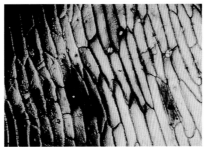
Red onion skin plain water at 125✕; enlarged.

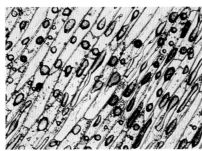
Red onion skin in salt solution at 125✕; enlarged.

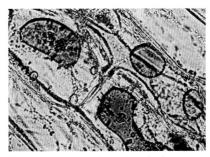
Red onion skin in salt solution at 312.5✕; enlarged.

SCIENCE FAIR

Use your microscope to examine onion skin cells that are placed in different concentrations of salt solutions. Observe the changes as they occur by pulling the salt water under the cover slip using a piece of paper towel (see Pulling a Stain). Place a few drops of salt water on one side of the cover slip and hold a corner of the paper towel near the other side of the cover slip. The salt water will move underneath. Watch the effect of the salt water as the changes occur. Will different strengths of salt water have the same effect? Does this effect occur in other plant samples also? Try making wet mounts of small pieces of *Elodia* or other aquarium plants to see the effects of salt water on them.

Onion Soup

Have you ever wondered why purple onions are a different color than yellow or white cooking onions? This is because purple onions contain a pigment called anthocyanin. Anthocyanin acts as an indicator. Indicators are compounds that change color when they are placed in acids or bases. Let's see how the purple onion can change colors.

You Will Need

→ raw purple onion

→ knife and tweezers

→ eyedropper and water

→ slides and cover slips

→ tissue or paper towel

→ vinegar

→ baking soda

→ measuring cup and tablespoon

→ microscope

What to Do

1. Cut a piece of a layer from a raw purple onion. Then cut it into ½ inch (1 cm) sections.

2. Remove a piece of the thin skin from the outer, convex side of the layer of purple onion by pulling it gently with tweezers. Cut the skin into two pieces, each about ¼ inch (6 mm) long.

3. Using two slides and two cover slips, make two wet mounts of the onion skin (see Making a Wet Mount, page 12).

4. Examine your first slide under the microscope, using both the low-power and high-power objectives.

5. Place a few drops of vinegar on one side of the cover slip and hold a corner of the paper towel near the other side of the cover slip. Do this in the same way you would pull a stain (see page 12). The vinegar will move underneath. Watch the effect of the vinegar on the onion skin under the microscope.

6. Examine your second slide under the microscope, using both the low-power and high-power objectives.

7. Dissolve a tablespoon (15 mL) of baking soda in ½ cup (125 mL) of warm water. Stir to dissolve completely. This is your baking soda solution.

8. Place a few drops of the baking soda solution on one side of the cover slip and hold a corner of the paper towel near the other side of the cover slip. Do this in the same way you would pull a stain. The baking soda solution will move underneath the cover slip, into the sample. Watch the effect of the baking soda solution on your onion skin sample under the microscope.

What Happened

In your onion skin samples in plain water, you saw the long, narrow onion skin cells. Inside the wall of each cell, there is a thin cell membrane, although it is too thin to see with a light microscope. The cell membrane contains the cytoplasm, or fluid inside the cell. The pigment (coloring substance) anthocyanin is in the cytoplasm. When you looked at the onion cells in each of the slides at the beginning of the experiment, you saw that they were purple. When the vinegar was added, the cells became more acid. As they became more acid, the onion skin turned a redder color. When the baking soda solution was added to a piece of onion skin in water, the cells became more basic. As they became less acid, they lost their reddish appearance and looked gray or purplish blue.

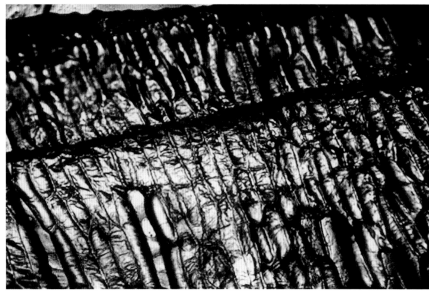
Red onion skin at 31.25✕; enlarged.

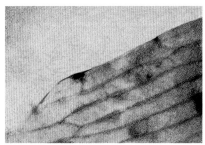
Red onion skin with baking soda (base) at 125✕; enlarged.

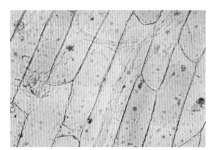
Red onion skin with baking soda at 312.5✕; enlarged.

ſCIENCE ƑAIR

Onion skin and other plants that contain indicators can be used to test materials for acidity. A good substitute for purple onion is purple cabbage. Chop up 2 cups (500 mL) of cabbage and pour 4 cups (1 L) of very hot water over the cabbage. Sieve out the cabbage, and use the colored water as an indicator to test materials. When you add an acid, your cabbage water will become red; when you add a base, your cabbage water will turn blue or green. You can even soak a coffee filter in the cabbage water, allow it to dry, and cut it into strips to use as indicator test strips.

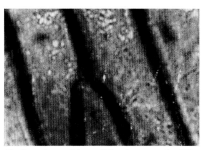
Red onion skin with vinegar (acid), at 312.5✕; enlarged.

Dew You Love Me? ⚠️

Some plants have a funny way of getting fed. While most plants do nothing about becoming dinner for insects, animals or even people, others turn the tables and make dinner of an insect. The Sundew is an example. It likes to trap insects on the shiny, sticky droplets on its leaves; then it digests the insects! The stinging nettle uses its weapons for defense, not for food. It has tiny stinging hairs on its leaves. When you touch a nettle, the hairs pierce your skin and give off a kind of acid juice, which can hurt, itch, or cause a rash. By examining these plants under a microscope, you can begin to see how plants go on the attack.

You Will Need

→ a Sundew, Venus's-flytrap, or butterwort—all insect-eating plants*

→ leaf of a stinging nettle or of another prickly plant, such as a thistle**

→ gloves

→ tweezers

→ jars or containers

→ sharp knife

→ slides

→ microscope

→ lamp

*You may need to get a sample of your insect-eating plant at a plant store.

**Wear gloves and long, thick pants when collecting prickly samples in the field, so the plants don't scratch your hands or legs.

What to Do

1. Wear gloves and carefully collect a small sample of a leaf of one of the above plants, using a tweezers. Don't touch the plant with your bare hands. Place each sample in its own jar or container.

2. Have an adult cut a small sample of each leaf and place each on a slide. If the sample is thin, make a wet mount (see page 12). If the sample is thick, place it on the slide and shine light on it from above; view it under low power only. Can you see what makes these plant leaves so different from other leaves?

3. Use tweezers to break off one of the long, sharp hairs on the stinging nettle; place it on a clean slide, without a cover slip. View it under the low-power objective. Can you see any liquid?

4. Use tweezers to squeeze the end of a Sundew hair. Smear the liquid at the end of the hair onto a slide and view it under high power. (See Making a Smear Slide on page 13.) What does the liquid look like under a microscope?

What Happened

You saw the stinging or sticking parts of the plants. The Sundew plants have leaves with long

Sundew at 60×; enlarged.

Sundew at 120×; enlarged.

Sundew at 120×; enlarged.

red-tipped hairs. When an insect lands on the plant, it becomes trapped in the sticky liquid on the tips of the hairs. The hairs bend inward, trapping the insect. The plant gives off a liquid that digests the insect and absorbs nutrients from the digested insect.

The stinging nettle and other similar plants have needlelike hairs on their leaves. The tips of these hairs are made of a hard, glassy material called silica. The plant oozes an irritating liquid from the tips of the hairs. When an animal touches the nettles or tries to eat them, the leaf hairs pierce the animal's skin, and the liquid the plant gives off causes itching.

ƒCIENCE ƑAIR

Get a Venus's-flytrap plant. Make a squash slide of a small piece of ground meat. Examine the meat slide under the low and medium-power objectives of your microscope. Collect a sample of liquid from the center of the plant, using an eyedropper. Carefully remove the cover slip and add a drop of the liquid you got from the plant to your meat sample. Leave it for a few minutes; then replace the cover slip and examine the slide under the microscope again. Check the slide every few minutses to see if there is any change in your meat sample.

Not-So-Dandy Lions

Every gardener knows how difficult it is to grow a weed-free lawn. Despite constant care and tending, weeds seem to spring up everywhere. Where do all the weeds come from? By examining the common dandelion, you can begin to understand how and why there are so many of them in lawns all over the world.

Gather several white dandelion heads and place them in an envelope or plastic bag to take home. Try to collect some flowers of some other kinds of weeds, also. Make sure to keep them in different bags or envelopes. If you know the plant's name, put a label in the bag so that you know which type of weed is inside.

You Will Need

→ several white dandelion heads, milkweed seed pods, and other fluffy weed flowers

→ letter envelopes or clear plastic bags

→ tweezers

→ water

→ slides and cover slips

→ eyedropper

→ microscope

→ pen and paper

What to Do

1. Use a pair of tweezers to pick a single piece or strand from a dandelion flower head, including a seed and its fluffy attachment.

2. Put the sample on a slide in a drop of water. Then lower a cover slip over the sample, trying not to trap any air bubbles.

3. Examine the different parts of the sample under low and high power. Compare the fluffy hairs with the seed.

4. Compare your first sample with the seeds of other seedball type weeds. Draw a picture of each to show the similarities and differences.

What Happened

You saw the seed and the attached parts that transport the seed through the air. The hairlike parts are a natural parachute. They are lightweight and shaped so that even a small breeze can cause them to break away from the weed and be carried to a new place, where they can grow. When the parachute lands, the rough edges of the parachute and seed help the seed stay anchored to the soil.

If you hold a fluffy white seedball in your hand, you will see why dandelions are so plentiful. Each ball contains hundreds of seeds, and each seed can become a new plant.

Dandelion seed at 250×; enlarged.

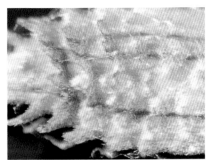

Dandelion seed at 500×; enlarged.

Dandelion seed "parachutes" at 60×; enlarged.

Dandelion seed "parachutes" at 500×.

SCIENCE FAIR

In a room with the doors and windows closed, use the air from a hair dryer to see how far seeds can travel. Which kinds of weed seeds travel the farthest? How does their shape affect the distance they travel? Make models of the different seed shapes and test them, in a kind of seed paper airplane race.

Getting to the Root of Things ⚠

By now you've had a chance to study several parts of a flowering plant: the pollen, the stem, the leaves, and the seeds. You've worked your way down to the roots. Roots are very important to plants. Without roots, the plant could not take in any water or nutrients which it needs to live. The roots anchor the plant to the soil, so that it does not blow away. Here's a simple way to grow some roots.

You Will Need

- ➜ onion
- ➜ wide-mouthed glass jar
- ➜ toothpicks
- ➜ water
- ➜ knife
- ➜ carrot
- ➜ microtome
- ➜ tweezers
- ➜ eyedropper
- ➜ slides and cover slips
- ➜ tincture of iodine
- ➜ microscope
- ➜ pen and paper
- ➜ paper towel

What to Do

Note: Roots are very fragile and damage easily. You must be careful not to squash them or hold them too tightly, as it will then be difficult to prepare a good slide.

1. Fill the glass jar one-third full with water. Stick three or four toothpicks into the onion, halfway up the onion, so that most of the toothpick is sticking out from the onion like the spoke on a wheel. Rest the toothpicks on the sides of the jar so the onion is hanging over the water, balanced on the toothpicks. The round bottom part of the onion should be in the water.

2. Place the jar in a warm, dark place for several days. You should begin to notice long, thin hairlike roots growing from the bottom of the onion. The top of the onion may start to show green sprouts.

3. When the roots are about 2 inches (5 cm) long, remove the onion from the jar and place it on your work table.

4. Use a kitchen knife to cut the ends of 2 roots from the onion. Return the onion to the jar of water. This will keep the roots wet in case you want to make more slides.

5. Have an adult prepare a piece of root by slicing a very thin ½ inch long (1 cm) section from the outside of the root, lengthwise from the tip of the root to the end. Use tweezers to carefully transfer the root sample to a slide. Make a wet mount of this section, following the instructions on page 12.

6. Examine your slide under both the low-power and high-power objectives. Make note of what the section looks like.

7. Now have an adult cut several cross-sections of the second root end you cut, using the microtome (see the instructions

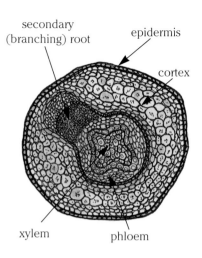

Cross-section of a root.

on using a microtome on page 11). Make the cross-sections as thin as possible. Try to get one cross-section from near the tip of the root.

8. Prepare wet mounts of cross-sections of the root, including one of the root tip. Stain one with iodine (see Pulling a Stain on page 12). Examine your slides under both the low-power and high-power objectives and make sketches of what they look like.

What Happened

When you look at the cross-section of the root, you see the outer layer, or epidermis, of the root on the outside of the cross-section. The epidermis is made up of small cells. Inside these

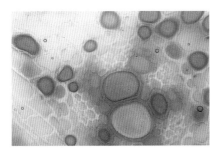
Cross-section of onion root at 312.5×; enlarged.

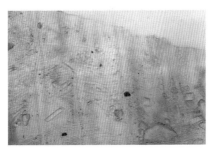
Longitudinal section of onion root at 312.5×; enlarged.

Onion root tip in cross section at 100×; enlarged.

cells are larger, light-colored cortex cells, which make up the bulk of the root. You probably saw larger round xylem cells and smaller round phloem cells also. The xylem cells are the ones through which the roots transport water into the plants. The phloem cells are the ones through which the roots trans-port nutrients from the soil into the plant. (We saw some of these earlier in Jack and the Beanstalk.) In the lengthwise (longitudinal) section of the root, the xylem cells look like long narrow boxes. When you looked at a cross-section from the tip of the root under high power (around 300 to 500×), you may have seen cells with dark blobs in their nuclei. These dark blobs are the chro-mosomes, which contain the information the plant needs to make new cells. The cells near the tip of the root are rapidly dividing to make new cells as the root grows longer.

SCIENCE FAIR

Compare the roots of different types of vegetables. Grow a few bean seeds in a damp paper towel and make a squash slide of the roots that grow out of the seeds. Try growing a carrot top with about ½ inch (1 cm) of carrot left below the top. Stand the carrot in a shallow dish of pebbles and water. Keep it moist and leave it in a dark place for a few weeks. When roots start to grow, cut a thin slice from the growing part and make it into a wet mount to view with your microscope.

A Close Shave

Trees are actually very large woody plants, which live for many years. Their trunks are really very thick stems. How can you find out what's really happening inside a tree? You obviously can't put a tree under a microscope, or can you? Here is an easy way to examine part of a tree, one that is probably at your fingertips!

You Will Need

➜ wooden pencil

➜ hand-held pencil sharpener or carrot scraper

➜ slide

➜ water

➜ cover slip

➜ microscope

What to Do

1. Use a pencil sharpener or carrot scraper to peel a thin shaving from the end of a pencil.

2. Place the shaving on a slide and make a wet mount of the shaving (see Making a Wet Mount, page 12).

3. View the slide under the microscope, using the low- and high-power objectives.

What Happened

Pencils are usually made from the wood of cedar trees. In your pencil shaving slide, you probably saw some of the wood cells (xylem) that make up the central, woody part of the tree. Like the ones in our photos, the cells are long and narrow, with thick cell walls. They function to transport water and minerals up the tree and also to support the tree. In

your pencil, all the cells are not alive, but in the actual tree, some cells are nonliving and some are living.

The tree grows from the cell division of the thin layer of cells near the bark called cambium. As it grows, the xylem cells are pushed toward the center. A tree thus grows in rings, inward. The cells produced in spring are larger than the ones produced in winter. Scientists can tell the age of a tree by counting the number of rings the tree has.

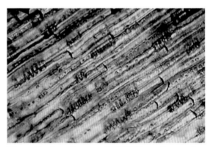

Pencil shavings at 125✕; enlarged.

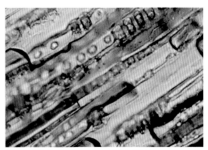

Pencil shavings at 312.5✕; enlarged.

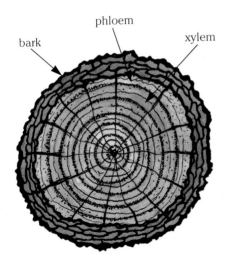

bark — phloem — xylem

Cross-section of a tree, showing annual rings.

ꟻCIENCE ꟻAIR

Look at some cells from another part of a tree. Ask an adult to help you to cut twigs from several kinds of trees, and shave off a small piece of bark with a carrot scraper from each. Make wet mounts of them and look at them under low power on the microscope. Compare them to each other, and to the pencil shaving. Record your findings. Note: The bark is an important protective layer of the tree. Never cut large pieces of bark from a tree, or a ring from all around a tree, or the tree could die.

FOOD

Most people don't associate microscopes and food. You may be surprised to learn that microscopes are used by scientists in the production of food products and the creation of new types of foods. Scientists also use microscopes to check foods for contaminants.

With your microscope, you can take a new look at things people eat and drink. You can study the lowly mushroom to learn about its structure or look at milk samples to see their fat globules. You can look at the various kinds of coffee using a microscope. Once you *get the idea, you'll find many interesting things as close as the fruit bowl. Next time someone says to you, "That's like comparing apples to oranges," you will be able to pull out a slide and really show them you know what that means!*

Webs and Gills ⚠

You Will Need

→ several different kinds of fresh mushrooms, including one with gills (see step 1)

→ sharp knife

→ slides and cover slips

→ microscope

→ labels and pencil

→ water

→ eyedropper

What do webs and gills have to do with mushrooms? It turns out that some mushrooms have webs and gills, but not the same kind as ducks and fish have. Underneath the cap of some mushrooms are gills that look like thin leaves of tissue. The gills are where these mushrooms grow spores. Mushrooms are fungi. Spores serve the same function as seeds in flowering plants. Under the right conditions, spores can grow into new mushrooms. Let's look at some mushrooms up close.

*Warning: Do not taste or eat any mushrooms that you have gathered from the garden or forest; they may be poisonous. Wash your hands and equipment with soap and water after this experiment and be sure to throw away any unknown mushrooms when you are done so they aren't mistaken for food.

What to Do

1. Get several different kinds of mushrooms, including one with gills, such as a Portobello or an ordinary brown or white mushroom from the grocery or vegetable store.

2. Have an adult slice a very thin piece of a mushroom gill with a knife.

3. Make a wet mount of the gill piece (see Making a Wet Mount on page 12).

4. Observe your slide under the microscope using the low-power and high-power objectives. Record your observations.

5. Make more slides using pieces of gills from other kinds of mushrooms. If the other mushrooms don't have gills, try to find the spore-bearing surface (maybe the underside of the cap) and make a sample of it.

6. Observe these slides using the low-power and high-power objectives. Compare the different mushroom samples. Record your observations.

What Happened

You may have seen spores growing on the gills, on knoblike structures called basidia. The spores are small roundish structures. Spores come in a variety of colors. The colors are often used as one clue to identify unknown mushrooms. The spores are easily removed from the basidia; you may have found them loose on your slide.

Mushrooms aren't plants. They don't have chlorophyll like plants, so they can't make their own food. What we call a mushroom is really the fruiting body that grows from the webs of threadlike structures (hyphae) that together are

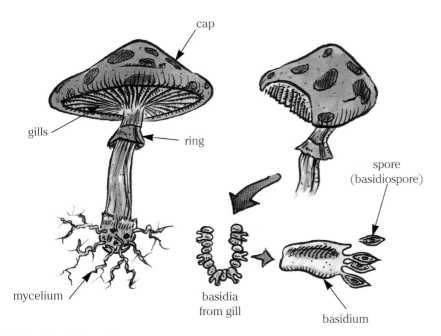

Parts of a gill mushroom.

called the mycelium. The parts of the mycelium underground absorb nutrients for the mushroom.

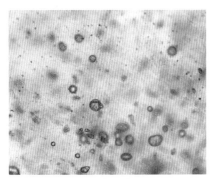

Mushroom gills showing spores at 125✕; enlarged.

Mushroom gills at 120✕; enlarged.

Mushroom gills at 500✕; enlarged.

∫CIENCE ℱAIR

Observe the spores of some other mushrooms. You can observe the spores easily by leaving the cap of the mushroom on a clean slide overnight in a warm place, with the spore-bearing surface (such as the gills) facing down. After a few hours, the mushroom will release some spores onto the slide. Make a wet mount of the spores and observe them.

Other types of fungi such as molds are also interesting to look at under the microscope. Grow some bread mold by dampening a slide of bread with water and sealing it in a plastic bag. Leave it in a warm place for several days until it grows mold. The mold will look like a colored smudge—perhaps green, white, or black—on the bread. Make a wet mount of the mold, using a pair of tweezers to transfer it to the slide. Make a slide of the mycelium of a mushroom and compare it to the bread mold.

Espresso Yourself

Many adults begin their day with a strong cup of coffee, or for that matter, several strong cups of coffee. There are many kinds or blends of coffee and different ways of preparing this drink. Sometimes chicory, an herb, and other additives are mixed with the ground coffee beans. Here is a way of studying the differences among various kinds of coffee.

You Will Need

→ one or two fresh coffee beans

→ one or two roasted coffee beans

→ hammer

→ aluminum foil

→ freeze-dried coffee crystals

→ ground coffee from a can or package

→ slides

→ tweezers

→ pen and paper

→ labels or tape

→ microscope

What to Do

1. Ask at a coffee store or grocery store for samples of fresh coffee beans, both unroasted and roasted. You will only need one or two of each kind of bean. Rub each bean between your fingers. What does it feel like?

2. Wrap each bean in a piece of aluminum foil. Use the hammer to crush the bean into tiny bits.

3. Use the tweezers to place a tiny sample of the coffee bean on a slide. Label the slide so that you know which sample you are looking at.

4. Carefully transfer the slide onto the stage of the microscope and secure it with the stage clips. Observe your slide using the low-power and high-power objectives.

5. Use a hammer to crush the freeze-dried coffee on a piece of aluminum foil. Place a tiny sample of this on a slide, using the tweezers. What do you see when you look at this slide with your microscope?

6. Prepare another slide by placing a small sample of ground coffee on the slide. How does this slide compare with the others?

What Happened

When you rubbed the coffee beans, they felt greasy. This is because the coffee beans have a tiny amount of oil in them. You should have been able to see the oil drops inside the cells of the coffee when it was under the microscope. Freeze-dried instant coffee has crystals

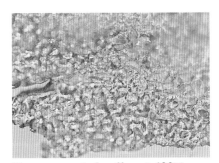
Raw, unroasted coffee at 400×; enlarged.

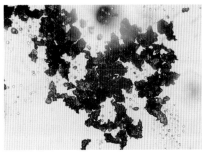
Roasted coffee at 100×; enlarged.

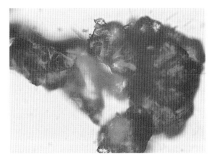
Instant coffee at 400×; enlarged.

but no cell structure. This is because of the way that this coffee was made. Freeze-dried coffee was made into a liquid and then processed into the crystalline form that people use.

Ground coffee can contain other foods. The most common additive is chicory. The chicory plant is pulled from the ground.

SCIENCE FAIR

Compare different brands of coffee. Does coffee from different countries look different under the microscope? Place a few drops of brewed coffee on a microscope slide and allow it to evaporate. How does this look?

Its roots are roasted and then ground up and added to coffee.

Any chicory that is in the coffee will look like long fibers.

Milk Shakes

The next time you are in a grocery store, take a look in the dairy section. You will notice there are different types of dairy products, including skim milk, 1% fat, 2% fat, and whole milk. You may also find buttermilk, sour cream, whipping cream, perhaps even goat's milk. Milk makes fascinating viewing under a microscope. Doing this experiment, you will be able to see the difference that the butter fat makes in the various kinds of milk.

You Will Need

→ a small amount of several types of milk

→ a small amount of vanilla ice cream

→ eyedropper

→ slides

→ cover slips

→ pen and paper

→ labels or tape

→ microscope

What to Do

1. Use the eyedropper to place a small drop of one of the kinds of milk on a slide.

2. Make a smear of the milk sample, following the instructions on making a smear slide on page 13.

3. Label the sample so that you know which type of milk you are looking at.

4. Observe your slide using the low-power and high-power objectives.

5. Note the size and number of the round, fat blobs, floating in the milk.

6. Make several sides using different kinds of milk, melted ice cream and imitation milk. Look at them in the same way as your first sample and record your observations.

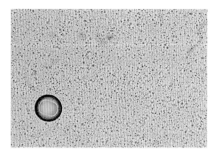

2% milk at 400×; enlarged. Large round circle is an air bubble.

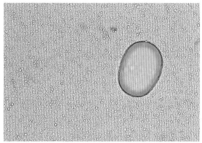

Whole milk at 400×; enlarged. Large round circle is an air bubble.

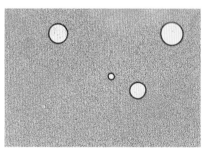

Half and half (milk with cream), at 100×; enlarged. Large round circles are air bubbles.

What Happened

If you looked at whole milk or ice cream, you probably saw a number of small round circles; they are fat globules. If you looked at skim milk, you didn't see fat globules. The larger circles you may have seen in any of the samples are air bubbles. (It is a good idea to create some air bubbles so that you can see how they are different from the fat globules. The air bubbles tend to be larger and have darker edges.) The fat globules are what makes the whole milk and the ice cream opaque or hard to see through. The skim milk is much more transparent and easy to see through.

ſCIENCE ƑAIR

Using your microscope, compare other dairy products, such as different brands of ice cream, for their fat content.

Comparing Apples to Oranges ⚠

Have you noticed that pears seem to taste gritty or grainy when you eat them? Apples, on the other hand, seem to be smooth-textured, even though they crunch in your teeth. Both have a different texture than an orange, grapefruit, or lemon. By examining these fruits under a microscope and comparing them to each other, you can explore some of their differences.

You Will Need

→ pear*

→ apple

→ citrus fruits: orange, lemon, or grapefruit

→ kitchen knife

→ microtome (see page 11)

→ tweezers

→ slides and cover slips

→ microscope

→ pen and paper

→ labels or tape

→ lens paper

*A not very ripe one works best.

What to Do

1. Use a kitchen knife to cut out a small piece of apple. Prepare a thin slice of this using your homemade microtome (see page 11).

2. Make a wet mount of the apple sample on a clean slide (see page 12 on making a wet mount). Label the slide.

3. Observe your slide using the low-power and high-power objectives. Record your observations.

4. Repeat the above steps using a pear. How does it look compared to the apple sample?

5. Cut a section of orange. Use tweezers to remove one of the small tear-shaped pieces of the orange fruit and use it to make a squash slide (see page 14). Label the slide.

6. View the slide as in step 3. How is the orange flesh different from that of the other fruits?

7. Repeat steps 5 and 6, taking a sample from a grapefruit and a lemon. How do they compare with the orange?

What Happened

You saw small dark grains, called stone cells, in the smooth background of the pear cells. They are the gritty parts you sometimes feel with your teeth when you bite into a pear. The apple sample had smooth, uniform cells with no grainy material. The orange, grapefruit, and lemon samples only showed a faint coloring; you may have seen the thin membrane that held in the juice.

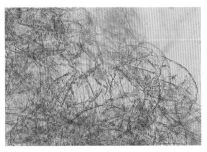

Micrograph of apple sample at 100X; enlarged.

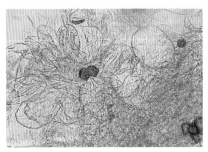

Micrograph of pear sample at 100X; enlarged.

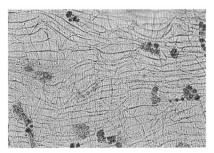

Micrograph of lemon section at 100X; enlarged.

Science Fair

Apples and pears turn brown when they are cut open and exposed to the air. Place a thin sample of an apple or a pear on a slide. Look at it under the microscope. Then leave the cover slip off so it is exposed to air. Watch the changes that occur. When your sample turns brown, look at your slide under the microscope to see how your sample is different than before it was exposed to air. Take a new sample. Brush a little lemon juice over it, and then expose it to air. Did the sample change color? What other fruit juices will stop the color change?

Peach Fuzz

Have you ever noticed how the skin of some fruits feels smooth, while the skin of others feels fuzzy? Do you hate the way peach skin feels against your tongue? It's time to examine just what makes a peach feel the way it does.

You Will Need
→ a peach, a nectarine, or an apricot

→ potato peeler or knife

→ tweezers

→ eyedropper

→ toothpick

→ slides and cover slips

→ water

→ microscope

→ pen and paper

What to Do

1. Peel a small, thin piece of skin from a fresh peach. Use the tweezers to place it on a slide.

2. Cover the skin with a drop of water; then lower the cover slip over the sample, trying not to trap any bubbles.

3. Observe your slide under the microscope, using the low- and high-power objectives.

4. Using a toothpick, gently scrape some of the fuzz from a peach and place this on another slide.

5. Cover this fuzz with a drop of water, then lower the cover slip the same way you did in step 2. Can you see the individual "hairs" of peach fuzz?

6. Try this experiment again, this time using a nectarine or an apricot. How does the skin of either of these fruits compare with that of the peach?

What Happened

You saw that the fuzz on these fruits looked like tiny "hairs" when observed through a microscope. The skin or epidermis of the fruit is made up of many tiny cells. Some of these cells have long, thin sections sticking out, which look like little hairs. Nectarine skin is much smoother than peach skin. It doesn't have hairlike cells. Apricots have skin that is fuzzy, but usually not as fuzzy as peach skin. Under the microscope, the surface of the apricot skin also shows the tiny "hairs," but they are shorter and farther apart than the ones on the peach.

Nectarine skin at 60×; enlarged.

Peach skin at 120×; enlarged.

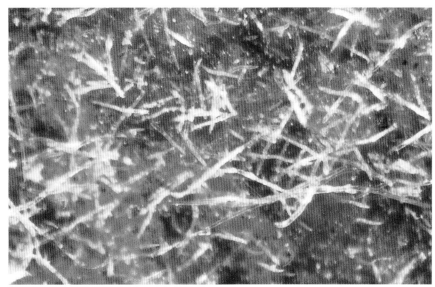
Peach skin at 500×; enlarged.

ЅCIENCE ҒAIR

How can you make a peach less fuzzy? Try rubbing the surface of the peach with different substances, such as a cloth or very fine sandpaper. Look at the surface of other fruits. Why do you think the peach has fuzz?

Spice Mélange

Spices and herbs are used today to give our foods tasty flavors, but in ancient times they were mainly used for religious purposes. The money that could be earned in the spice trade sent many explorers voyaging afar. Besides smelling good, spices are interesting to look at under the microscope.

You Will Need

➜ ⅛ teaspoon of any of the following spices and herbs: ground nutmeg, cinnamon, dill weed, oregano, red pepper or paprika, thyme, mace, curry, or different kinds of tea leaves

➜ slides

➜ cover slips

➜ labels

➜ pencil

➜ microscope

What to Do

1. For each spice or herb, place a tiny amount on its own slide.

2. Lower a cover slip over each slide and label each slide with the name of the sample.

3. View the samples under the low- and high-power objectives.

4. Try to get a sample of each of the things you are examining in its whole form. Look for a red pepper, a piece of cinnamon, a piece of dill weed, a nutmeg seed, etc., and compare each to the ground sample.

What Happened

Many spices and herbs are made of plant materials. Some of the things you looked at, such as thyme and oregano, are made from the dried leaves of plants. Others, like cinnamon, are made from the dried bark of a tree. Some, like red pepper, are made from dried fruit. There are even some mixtures, such as curry powder, which are made from a number of different spices. When you look at the different slides and see some that are similar in appearance, it's likely that they are probably from the same part of related plants.

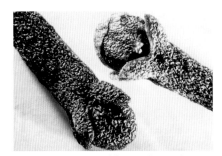

Whole cloves at 60✕; enlarged.

Whole cloves at 102✕; enlarged.

Ground oregano at 250×; enlarged.

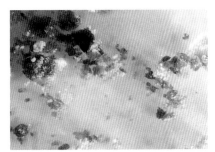

Paprika at 250×; enlarged.

Parsley at 120×; enlarged.

Lemon pepper (pepper, lemon peel, and other spices) at 250×; enlarged.

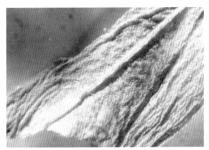

Tarragon at 120×; enlarged.

Tarragon at 250×; enlarged.

ƒCIENCE ƑAIR

Compare different types of salt, such as sea salt, coarse kosher salt, and iodized table salt by looking at them with your microscope. Note the similarities and any differences. Look at sugar: brown sugar, confectioners' sugar, and sugar substitutes. Compare your results.

EVERYDAY THINGS

In the movie Honey, I Shrunk the Kids, the children were reduced to the size of tiny specks. From their new viewpoint, ants appeared as large as horses; blades of grass became trees, and a breakfast cereal became a personal flotation device. Imagine what it would be like if you were that small! There's no way to make yourself that tiny, but you can make small things bigger so you can study them. Using a microscope, you can get a close-up view of some of the things that you handle everyday. You'll be surprised to discover how they look when they are 450 times bigger than real life.

Sand Castles

It's always fun to make mud-pies. They never need baking and they generally are low in calories. Sand castles are fun to build too, but they fall apart when they dry. If you ever made an animal or bowl out of potter's clay, you know it's plastic and sticky when moist, but keeps its shape when it dries. In fact, when clay is baked, it keeps its shape permanently. Mud, clay, and sand may seem similar, but let's look at them under the microscope to see what they look like close up.

You Will Need

➜ 5 slides

➜ water

➜ 4 cover slips

➜ ¼ teaspoon (1 mL) potter's clay

➜ ¼ teaspoon (1 mL) mud

➜ ¼ teaspoon (1 mL) sand
➜ ¼ teaspoon (1 mL) garden soil

➜ microscope

➜ toothpicks

➜ paper and pencil

What to Do

1. Use a toothpick to place a small amount of potter's clay on a slide, add a drop of water, and make a smear slide (see instructions for making a smear slide on page 13). Lower the cover slip over the sample, being careful not to trap any air bubbles.

2. View the slide under the low- and high-power objectives. Do a drawing of what you see at each magnification or explain it in words.

3. Place a small amount of sand on another slide; you don't need a cover slip. View it under the low-power objective. Record your findings on your paper.

4. Place a small amount of mud on a slide with a toothpick, add a drop of water, and make a smear slide as you did for the clay. View the mud under the low- and high-power objectives.

5. Use a small amount of soil to make a slide as you did with the sand. View this slide under the low-power objective and record your findings.

What Happened

The grains of sand were quite large and looked like crystals under the microscope. You may have found sand grains all of one kind, as in our photo, or sand with many different kinds of particles, even tiny shell pieces. Sand is mostly the result of the weathering of rocks containing quartz, with small amounts of other minerals such as magnetite, mica, and feldspar. The rocks are gradually broken into smaller pieces by wind, rain, and changes in temperature. The soil had a variety of particles of many sizes and shapes, including grains of sand. You probably found bits of grass and other plant matter in the soil. Mud, which is soil plus water, probably looked similar to the soil. The potter's clay probably had very tiny particles that were quite similar to each other.

Potter's clay also is the result of the weathering of rocks, mostly feldspar. It has been sieved and washed to give it an even texture. Other things are added to it to give it plasticity. Depending on the other things in the clay besides feldspar, the clay may be red, yellow, gray, or another color. Because of the way the tiny particles of clay are arranged, they tend to stick together. This is why the potter's clay dries in the shape in which you mold it.

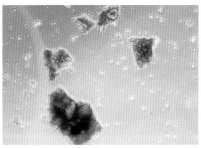
Potter's clay at 200✕; enlarged.

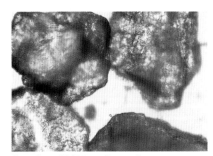
Sand at 200✕; enlarged.

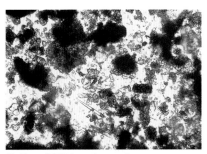
Soil at 200✕; enlarged.

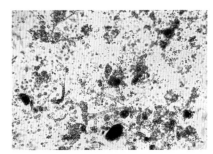
Mud at 200✕; enlarged.

SCIENCE FAIR

Get samples of sand or clay from several sources. Compare them to each other with your microscope. Record your observations. Visit a pottery studio and find out how the things that potters add to clay change its qualities. Get samples of each and look at them under the microscope.

A Bright Idea ⚠

Light bulbs are something we take for granted, at least until they burn out, leaving us in the dark. Many scientists, starting with Humphrey Davy in 1802, tried to invent an electric light by passing an electrical current through a thin piece of a substance to heat it enough to glow, giving off light. The light bulb was perfected by Thomas Alva Edison in 1879. He took a coil of carbonized cotton thread, placed it in a glass globe, and removed most of the air. He then ran an electric current through the coil and it glowed, or was incandescent. (An English inventor, Joseph Wilson Swan, had independently been working on almost the same thing, and they ended up jointly marketing electric light bulbs.) In the early 1900s, other inventors used tungsten to replace the carbonized thread as the thread-like element (filament) that got heated. Let's look at the filament of an incandescent light bulb close up to see how it works.

You Will Need

➜ a burned-out incandescent light bulb*

➜ 2 thick paper bags

➜ hammer

➜ masking tape

➜ tweezers

➜ slide

➜ microscope

➜ adult helper

*Do not use a fluorescent or halogen bulb. They contain gases that aren't good to breathe in.

What to Do

1. Place the light bulb inside a paper bag and put both inside another paper bag. Seal the bag. Have an adult break the light bulb by tapping the bulb through the bag with a hammer. Listen carefully as the bulb is broken and note any unusual sounds.

2. Have an adult use tweezers to remove the filament from the light bulb; it looks like a tiny coil of metal wire. Safely dispose of the broken glass in another sealed paper bag.

3. Tape each end of the filament to a slide.

4. Place the slide on the microscope stage and shine a light on it from above.

5. View the filament under both low- and medium-power objectives.

What Happened

When the bulb was broken, you may have heard a *whoosh* sound. This was caused by air moving into the vacuum of the broken light bulb. When the light bulb was made, the air inside was removed and it was sealed. Under the microscope, you were able to see the tungsten coil that is the filament. When the filament was whole, an electric current ran through it and heated it enough to make it glow, about 4500°F (2600°C). In the area where the filament burned out, the surface was rough and irregular. In the burned-out part of the filament, the tungsten became a vapor, which broke the electrical circuit. That's why the light bulb stopped working.

Light bulb filament at 500×; enlarged.

SCIENCE FAIR

Using your microscope, compare the filament in your burned-out light bulb to the filament in an unused bulb. How are they different? Look at some filaments from bulbs with different wattages. Record your findings.

A Flaky Experiment

If you have ever looked at a snow crystal that fell on your hand or your sleeve, you may have noticed its symmetrical shape. Some snow crystals are flat; others are thin and wispy. All of them are beautiful. Did

you ever wonder how they get their shapes? Grab your mittens and your supplies on the next snowy day, and let's look at some close up. You are in for a treat.

You Will Need

→ small piece of black construction paper or black velvet*

→ scissors

→ falling snow

→ microscope

→ flashlight

→ camera attachment to microscope (optional)

→ paper and pencil

→ helper

*It should be small enough to fit on your microscope stage.

What to Do

1. Place the construction paper or black velvet in the freezer and leave it there for at least an hour.

2. Take your microscope outside or place it near an open window. If your sample gets warm, it will melt.

3. Catch individual snow crystals as they fall on the black paper or velvet. Immediately place this on your microscope stage and view the sample, using the low-power objective. Have a helper shine a flashlight onto the stage to better light your sample.

4. Draw a sketch of the crystals or use the camera to record the different samples. Did you find any that were identical?

5. Dry your microscope thoroughly if you have taken it outside.

What Happened

Each crystal had its own unique shape. You may have found 6-sided plate shapes, needle shapes, columns, or more irregular shapes. The shape of the crystals is determined by several things, including the temperature in the clouds where the crystals were formed and how much moisture was in the air. When the temperature is around the freezing point of water (32°F or 0°C), snow crystals usually join together to form snowflakes. The 6-sided shape of many snow crystals is a result of the way the molecules of water join together when they crystallize. How snow crystals form is still being studied by scientists.

SCIENCE FAIR

Look at the snow crystals that fall on a warmer day and compare them to the crystals that fall on a colder day. Sketch them and measure the size of the flakes. Are the shapes and sizes of the crystals the same on both days?

Sweet Music

If you play guitar, violin, or any other stringed instrument, you know that each string has a different thickness. Strings that are thicker produce notes that are lower in tone than strings that are thinner. After you use them for a while, strings break. Try to get some old strings from a friend who plays an instrument or a store that sells musical instruments, and then let's examine some under the microscope to see what they are made of and why strings break with wear.

You Will Need

➜ small pieces of different kinds of strings from musical instruments

➜ scissors

➜ tweezers

➜ cellophane tape

➜ slide

➜ microscope

What to Do

1. Trim the string so that it can fit on a slide. If you have an old string, try to cut a sample from a part that is worn. To make viewing easier, tape one end of the string to the slide. Use tweezers to unravel or pick apart the unattached end of the string if it is made of more than one layer.

2. Use a desk lamp to light the string from above. View the string using the low-power objective.

3. Look at the next sample of string using the same technique.

What Happened

Some instrument strings are made up of a single nylon strand. Other strings have an inner core of several nylon strands wrapped in an outer layer of metal. Some strings are made of a strand of metal such as steel. Some are made of gut. If you had any wrapped strings, you could see the fibers inside the wrapped string. You could

see the worn-out area, perhaps with some broken fibers or wrapping. Strings wear when they are continually stressed. Stress happens when the strings are stretched and also each time they are strummed, bowed, or plucked. Each time you use the instrument, you damage the string a little bit. Eventually the string will break.

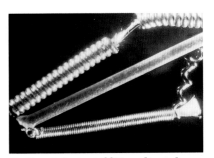

Guitar strings at 60×; enlarged.

SCIENCE FAIR

Compare several different kinds of guitar string that are for the same note and instrument. Test to see if a more complex or expensive string lasts longer under normal use. Interview musicians to ask them why they use certain strings.

Incriminating Evidence

Forensic scientists working with the police use microscopes to help them solve crimes. Clues such as hair, fingerprints, bits of fibers from clothes, and soil are collected and can be analyzed using a microscope. Special microscopes are used by law enforcement agencies to examine bullets, to determine whether they were fired from a particular gun. With a few pieces of cellophane tape and your microscope, you too can be a detective and examine clues around you.

You Will Need

→ cellophane tape

→ cover slips and slides

→ scissors

→ microscope

→ labels or adhesive tape

→ pencil and paper

→ coins and objects with rough surfaces

What to Do

1. Cut a few pieces of cellophane tape that are 1 inch (2.5 cm) long and stick each to a rough or uneven surface such as a coin or a piece of wood, a wicker basket, a carpet, or sandpaper. Press the tape firmly in place to get a clear impression.

2. Cut each piece of tape into two ½-inch-long (1 cm) sections. Place each piece of tape, sticky side down, on its own cover slip. Place each cover slip on a slide with the tape next to the slide. Label one slide in each pair with the source of the sample.

3. Examine the slides under low and high power. Try to match the unlabeled sample to its labeled half.

What Happened

Each surface made its own special pattern on the tape. You could match the pairs of samples by matching the slides by matching the patterns. The tape has adhesive on it, which picked up some markings from the rough surface.

Imprint of polar bear on tape, from Canadian coin, at 31.25✕; enlarged.

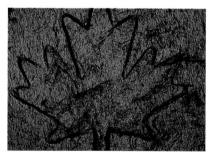

Imprint of maple leaf on tape, from Canadian coin, at 31.25✕; enlarged. Photographed with a blue filter.

*S*CIENCE *F*AIR

Crime lab scientists are sometimes asked to examine tooth marks and compare them to people's teeth. The shape and arrangement of teeth are one way of identifying a person. Use a scissors to cut a piece of foam that will fit into your mouth from a Styrofoam plate. It should be big enough to reach back and across to most of your teeth (about 2½ × 2 inches or 6 × 5 cm).

Place the foam between your upper and lower teeth and bite down on, but not through, the plate. Remove the plate from your mouth, rinse with clean water, and allow it to dry. Examine the tooth marks with a magnifying glass or with your microscope under low power. You have made a dental impression. Try making dental impressions of several people and comparing them.

A Good Impression ⚠

In Incriminating Evidence, we learned one way of making a surface print. Surface prints are helpful for looking at samples that are too thick for the light to pass through. Here are some other ways to make surface prints, using nail polish.

You Will Need

→ sharp knife

→ clear nail polish

→ thick flower petal or leaf*

* A petal from a rose or iris, or a thick leaf will work well.

→ tweezers

→ slide

→ microscope

→ pencil and paper

→ lamp

What to Do

Have an adult cut a small piece of flower petal or leaf. Place this on a slide. Light it from above with the lamp, and view it under the low-power objective. Make a drawing of what it looks like, or describe it in words.

Print method 1

1. Apply a layer of nail polish to the surface of another petal or leaf. Allow the polish to completely dry.

2. Use the tweezers to pull the dried layer of nail polish off the leaf or petal. Don't worry if you can't remove all the polish; you will only need a small section.

3. Place the section of nail polish on the slide, smooth side down, and view the sample under the low- and high-power objectives. Set the slide aside.

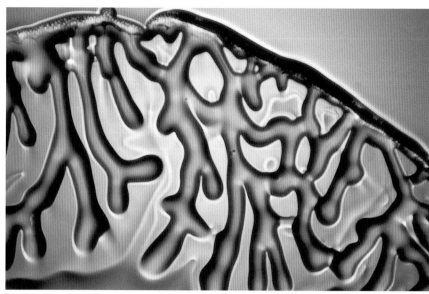

Nail polish imprint of hydrangea petal at 31.25✕; enlarged.

Print method 2

1. Coat a small area in the middle of a third microscope slide with a thin layer of nail polish.

2. Wait until the polish is sticky, but not yet dry. Press a flower petal onto the surface of the polish, and lift the petal off, leaving an impression.

3. Allow the slide to dry. View the nail polish impression under the low- and high-power objectives.

What Happened

You made impressions of the petal or leaf. In Print Method 1, the nail polish coated the sur-

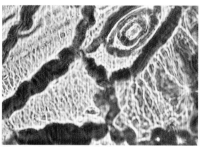

Peel of nail polish from geranium petal, at 312.5✕; enlarged.

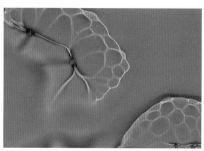

Nail polish imprint of hydrangea petal at 312.5✕; enlarged.

face and seeped into all the cracks in the sample. When you removed the hardened polish, it showed all the details in reverse. The parts that were low in the sample were high in the print. If you used a rose petal, you can see why rose petals appear to be velvety. In Print Method 2, the petal left an impression of its reverse in the wet nail polish.

SCIENCE FAIR

Make impressions of the top surface and the bottom surface of a leaf. Do you see any structures in your print of the bottom surface that are different from those you find on the top? Try to identify the structures, using diagrams of a leaf from a book.

A Shot in the Dark

If you compare a photograph you've taken to the film negative from which it was made, you're in for a surprise. If you look at the negative of a black-and-white picture, you see that everything is reversed. The things that in the print are white appear dark on the negative. The things that are black appear clear on the negative. A color negative is even more peculiar: The blue balloons you see on a print look yellow on the negative; red flowers look green on the negative; and the film itself is a kind of tea color. Let's explore some negatives and prints under the microscope to see what we can learn.

You Will Need

→ black-and-white negatives

→ color negatives

→ photographs made from the above negatives (if possible)

→ microscope

→ lamp

What to Do

1. Place the black-and-white negative you wish to view on the stage and secure it with the stage clips. (You don't need a slide, but if it curls up, you can put a slide on top to flatten it.)

2. Look at the black-and-white negative under the low- and high-power objectives. See if you can find any tiny dark grains.

3. Place the black-and-white photograph on the stage and secure it with the stage clips.

4. Look at the black-and-white photograph under the low-power objective, using the lamp to light it from above. Compare the negative to the photograph.

5. Place the color negative on the stage and secure it with the stage clips.

6. Look at the color negative under the low- and high-power objectives. Compare the color negative to the black-and-white negative.

7. Place the color photograph on the stage and secure it with the stage clips. Use the lamp to light it from above.

8. Look at the color photograph using the low-power objective. Compare the color negative to the color photograph.

What Happened

On the black-and-white negative, you saw a grainy surface in which some areas were darker than others. These grains are tiny silver particles. Black-and-white film is made with a layer of crystals of a silver compound, silver bromide, which is sensitive to light. When a bright or light-colored object reflects light into the camera, it hits the film and causes a reaction in the silver bromide. When the film is placed in a developer solution, the silver bromide crystals that were struck by light form black grains of metallic silver that stay on the film. In the film's processing, the parts of the silver bromide that weren't exposed to light are washed away, leaving a clear place.

When a print is made, the negative is placed over a light-sensitive piece of paper. Light is shined through the negative onto the paper. The parts of the negative that are dark block out the light, so those areas of the paper beneath the dark parts of the negative aren't exposed to light. They come out white in the print. The parts of the negative that are clear don't block out the light, and so the light-sensitive chemicals in the paper are exposed to light, and come out dark when the print is developed.

When you looked at the color print film under the

microscope, you probably saw areas of color with a very fine grain. Color film is made of three light-sensitive layers. Each layer is sensitive to a different color of light: blue, green, or red. There are light-sensitive particles of silver in each layer of color film. During film processing, dyes are attached to the silver particles that were exposed to light and the silver is then dissolved, leaving behind the dyes. Each layer of the negative ends up having the color of the opposite (complement) of the color that will print.

Color photo of a shirt at 60×; enlarged.

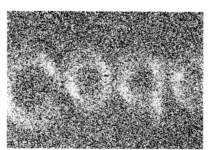
Black-and-white negative of a label at 500×; enlarged.

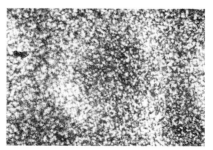
Black-and-white negative of a label at 312.5×; enlarged.

SCIENCE FAIR

Project 1. Make microscope slides of pictures from different printed sources, such as magazines and newspapers. Look at the slides under the microscope and compare the sizes of the dots you see. Do newspaper pictures have larger dots than magazine photos? Are the dots in the pictures on your slides larger than the ones you saw in your photographs or negatives? Project 2. Compare negatives of several speeds of film. Does 100 ASA film have larger or smaller silver particles than 200 ASA or 400 ASA film? How does the particle size affect the sharpness of the print?

Hidden Pictures

You probably handle some kind of money each day. Little did you know that this money contains tiny pictures, numbers, and designs, hidden on each bill and on some coins. This experiment is both educational and fun; it will also test your observation skills.

You Will Need

➜ a U.S. $1 bill or a Canadian or U.S., $5, $10, or $20 bill and a U.S. penny, or money from other countries

➜ microscope

➜ lamp

➜ pen and paper

What to Do

1. Place a U.S. penny, tail side up, on the microscope stage. Observe the center of the Lincoln Memorial, using the low-power and medium-power objectives. Use a lamp to light the sample from above. What did you find inside the Memorial?

2. Place each bill on the stage in turn, and secure it with the stage clips. View the bill while slowly moving it around under the lens. Did you find anything unusual?

3. Keep a record of which "hidden" words or symbols you find on each sample.

4. Try this again, using money from other countries. Do these bills also contain hidden pictures?

What Happened

There was a tiny man inside the Lincoln Memorial on the U.S. penny. You probably found tiny words hidden in the circle around the President on the U.S. $10 and $20 bill. If you were using Canadian money, you found that the clock on the tower on the $5 bill was set at 10 minutes to 2:00. You also saw that the wavy colored lines on the Canadian bills were not solid, but were, in fact, words. Countries place words or designs on their currency to prevent people from photocopying or printing fake money. In addition, magnetic inks and special paper are used, so that police and governments can tell the difference between real and forged money.

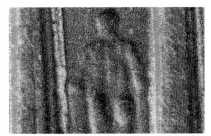
Lincoln on U.S. penny at 500✕; enlarged.

Canadian $20 bill at 120✕; enlarged.

SCIENCE FAIR

Compare currencies from different countries. Which country has the most hidden things in its bills? Which the least? Write to the government of these countries and find out how many counterfeit bills are discovered each year. Is there a relationship between these two things?

Glossary

anatomy: 1. a branch of biology that studies the structure of animals or plants. 2. the structural makeup of an organism or any of its parts.

alkaline (basic): having the properties of a base.

anthocyanin: a group of pigments (coloring substances) that causes most of the red and blue colors in leaves and flowers. Anthocyanin becomes reddish in an acid and violet or blue when placed in an alkaline (basic) solution. Anthocyanin is contained in purple onions.

arm: the curved part of the microscope that holds the tube in place over the stage and base.

bacteria (singular, **bacterium):** Tiny (0.2–10 μ m) one-celled living things in the Monera kingdom. Some bacteria cause diseases. Some break down other living things. Bacteria are usually identified by shape, such as bacilli (rod-shaped bacteria), cocci (round), and spirilla (spiral-shaped).

base: 1. the heavy bottom part of the microscope. 2. a bitter-tasting substance that can react with an acid to form a salt.

basidium (plural, **basidia):** a spore-bearing part that is typical of a group of fungi (Basiomycetes) that includes mushrooms. The basidia are located on the gills of some mushrooms.

binocular: a device that requires the use of both eyes at the same time.

cardiac muscle: a special kind of muscle found in the heart.

cartilage: gristle: a tough, resilient, elastic connective tissue found mainly in joints and tubular structures of animals. Cartilage acts as a support and cushion to other tissues. The skeleton of an embryo is mostly cartilage, which is gradually replaced by bone as it grows to adulthood.

cell: the smallest unit of a living thing that is capable of functioning on its own.

cell membrane: the thin boundary layer covering all cells, which controls the entering and leaving of substances into and out of the cell.

chondrocyte (from Gr. **chondros,** groats, and *kytos*, a hollow cell): cartilage cell, which occupies a lacuna (space) in a cartilage matrix.

chromosomes: threadlike structures in the nucleus of the cell that carry the information for making new living things.

cilia (plural of *cilium*, Latin for eyelash)*:* fine moveable hairlike extensions of a cell's surface that are present on some cells.

coarse adjustment knob: the large knob on the side of the microscope used to rapidly adjust the focus.

cortex cells: large light-colored cells that make up most of the root of a plant.

cotyledon: the seed leaf or first leaf or leaves that form when a plant grows from a seed.

cytoplasm: the fluid inside a cell between the cell membrane and the nucleus. The cytoplasm contains the water, the cytoskeleton, and cell structures.

diaphragm: the part of the microscope used to adjust the amount of light shining through a sample.

dicot (dicotyledon): a plant that has two cotyledons (seed leaves).

erythrocytes: red blood cells.

eyepiece: the lens system of the microscope closest to your eye.

fermentation: breakdown of complex compounds by bacteria or yeasts.

fertilization: process of the union of cells from two parents, which begins the development of a new individual.

fibers: threads, or structures that look like threads.

field of view: the area of a slide you can see through the eyepiece.

filament: 1. a single thread or threadlike object. 2. the fine metal wire in a light bulb that gives off light when electricity runs through it.

gene: a unit of heredity that occupies a particular place on a chromosome.

germinate: to start developing or growing.

gills: 1. the breathing apparatus of water-breathing animals. 2. the fine netlike structures used by fish and aquatic animals to take in oxygen. 3. the part of some mushrooms, under the cap, where the spores develop.

heart: a hollow, muscular organ that receives blood from the veins and pushes it into the arteries.

impression: a copy of the surface features of an object, made by pressure.

leukocytes: white blood cells.

marrow: yellow or red substance inside the hard sections of bones. The red marrow produces red blood cells and platelets and some white blood cells. The yellow marrow stores fat.

matrix: a substance between other cells in which they are embedded (for example, in cartilage).

microfossil: a fossil that can be studied only microscopically, whether it is the remains of a whole or part of a specimen.

Monera: biological group of simple organisms that includes bacteria and blue-green algae.

monocots (monocotyledons): a group of flowering plants, including grasses and lilies, that produce embryos having a single seed leaf (cotyledon).

muscle: 1. one of the tissues or organs of an animal's body that can contract, by which movement of various parts is caused. 2. a tissue consisting of specialized contractile cells. There are three basic kinds of muscle: cardiac (heart), skeletal, and smooth (visceral).

mushroom: a large fleshy or woody fungus. Some mushrooms are edible and some are poisonous.

mycelium: the mass of threadlike tubes that makes up the underground part of the mushroom.

myofibril: basic unit of muscle; a very small, threadlike structure made of complex proteins that is found lengthwise in skeletal or car-diac muscle fibers. It is made up of overlapped thin and thick myofilaments.

myofilaments: rows of tiny muscle filaments that slide past each other when muscles contract.

nitrogen-fixing bacteria: bacteria that take in nitrogen gas from the air and change it into a form of nitrogen that plants can use.

objectives: the parts of the microscope at the bottom of the tube that are closest to the sample. Each objective has a lens and a tubelike holder, the mount.

opaque: not allowing any light to pass through.

organ: a group of specialized tissues performing one main function.

phloem: the food-conducting vascular tissues in some plants.

photosynthesis: the process by which green plants produce food from water and carbon dioxide, using sunlight for energy.

pigment: a substance that gives color to a plant, animal, or other material.

plasma: the straw-colored liquid in which blood cells and platelets are suspended.

plastic (adj.): easily bent, folded, or twisted.

platelets: small, colorless irregularly shaped cell fragments found in blood, where they function in clotting. Platelets are ½ to ⅓ the size of red blood cells.

pollen tube: an outgrowth of a pollen grain, which the pollen grain produces to allow it to fertilize an ovum (egg).

revolving nosepiece: rotatable part of the microscope, which holds the objectives, which can be rotated into place as needed.

sample: an object or part of an object you wish to study or observe.

skeletal muscle: muscle used for voluntary movement of the body parts.

slide: 1. the thin, rectangular piece of glass on which a sample is placed for viewing. 2. the sample prepared for viewing on such a piece of glass.

smooth muscle: muscle found in the lining of blood vessels, internal organs, skin, and the excretory system. Smooth muscle has no cross-striations.

specimen: a portion of a material used for examination; a sample.

spicules: crystalline structures that form part of the skeletons of some sponges.

spongin: a protein that is the main part of the flexible fibers in the skeletons of some natural sponges.

stage: the flat surface of the microscope on which you place your slide.

stage clips: metal clips that hold the slide in place on the microscope stage.

striated: marked by stripes or lines.

symbiosis: a relationship of two unlike living things where one or both benefit and neither is harmed.

tissue: 1. a group of cells that perform the same function. 2. a soft paper used for cleaning slides, mopping up excess water, etc.

transparent: allowing light to pass through.

tube: the tube-shaped part of the microscope, which holds the nosepiece and objective lenses at one end and the eyepiece or ocular at the other end.

wattage: a measurement of electrical power.

weathering: the action of the weather (sun, wind, rain, freezing, and heating) that changes the shape and form of rocks and other exposed materials on the Earth's surface, breaking them down.

xylem: tubelike plant tissues that transport water and minerals, which also provide support for the plant.

Index